12-WEEK
FITNESS JOURNAL

12

WEEK

FITNESS JOURNAL

THE ULTIMATE PLANNER AND DAILY TRACKER
TO MEET YOUR FITNESS GOALS

ROCKRIDGE
PRESS

Maintaining a fitness journal will help you set goals, keep track of your progress, and see firsthand how well you're sticking to a steady exercise routine and diet plan. You'll have all the information you need to assess your current workout and make changes when necessary.

GETTING STARTED

Date: MARCH 23

FITNESS

GOALS:

LOSE 30 LBS.

SHED AT LEAST 5% OF MY BODY FAT.

PLAN:

WORK OUT EVERY MUSCLE GROUP AT

   LEAST ONCE A WEEK.

DO 3–5 SETS AND 8–10 REPS.

WORK OUT FOR 45 MINS–1 HOUR

NUTRITION

GOALS:

KEEP CALORIE COUNT UNDER 1200.

AVOID PROCESSED FOODS.

PLAN:

FOLLOW A LOW–CARB DIET.

EAT GOOD CARBS AND HEALTHY FATS.

EMPTY FRIDGE AND PANTRY OF ALL

   PROCESSED FOODS.

You can list your starting weight, measurements, daily targets, and any specific exercise goals. Fill in only the sections that are important for meeting your goals. Remember to set goals that are both challenging but realistic and attainable within the 12-week period.

STARTING STATS

BODY WEIGHT & MEASUREMENTS

	Current	Goal
Weight	187	150
Body Fat %	30%	22%
Upper Arms	—	—
Chest	40 IN	38 IN
Waist	35 IN	29 IN
Hips	—	—
Thighs	—	—
Calves	—	—

CARDIO

1-MILE RUN	12 MINS	9 MINS
TREADMILL SPEED	5.0	8.0

STRENGTH

PLANK	15 SECS	60 SECS
PUSH-UPS	15	25

NOTES:

DAILY TARGETS

Servings of Fruits/Veggies

6

Calories

1200

Carbs

30 GRAMS

Fat

135 GRAMS

Protein

100 GRAMS

Cups of Water

12

Hours of Sleep

8

Other: VIT D

400 IU

Other:

You can fill this in with any other information you'd like to track, such as sodium and cholesterol counts or vitamin and supplement intake.

WEEK 1 FITNESS PLAN

Dates: MARCH 23 to MARCH 29

	STRENGTH	CARDIO	CLASS / OTHER
MONDAY	CORE CRUNCHES, CHAIR LEG RAISE, OBLIQUE LEG RAISE	TREADMILL INTERVAL WORKOUT (30 MINS)	
TUESDAY	REST DAY		
WEDNESDAY	UPPER BODY SHOULDER PRESS, SIDE LATERAL RAISE, BICEP CURLS, TRICEP DIPS	TREADMILL TEMPO WORKOUT (30 MINS)	
THURSDAY	REST DAY		
FRIDAY	LEGS + BUTT BARBELL DEADLIFT, GLUTE BRIDGE, REVERSE LUNGE, CALF RAISE	TREADMILL TEMPO WORKOUT (30 MINS)	
SATURDAY			STRETCHING
SUNDAY			STRETCHING

In the beginning, you can start with the exercises you already know to develop a full-body routine. As you get confident with those movements, you can add or modify exercises for variety.

WEEK 1 MEAL PLAN

	BREAKFAST	LUNCH	DINNER	SNACKS
MONDAY	Breakfast casserole	Chicken skewers with green salad	Pork chile verde	Protein pumpkin latté
TUESDAY	Breakfast casserole (leftover)	Chicken skewers with green salad (leftover)	Pork chile verde (leftover)	Protein bar
WEDNESDAY	Breakfast casserole (leftover)			Greek yogurt with granola
THURSDAY	Raspberry-orange shake			Greek yogurt with granola
FRIDAY	Raspberry-orange shake	Crispy chicken with quinoa salad (leftover)	Grilled steak with spinach salad	Protein bar
SATURDAY	Banana pancakes	Crispy chicken with quinoa salad (leftover)	Turkey breast with beet salad	Peach Shake
SUNDAY	Peach shake	Broiled salmon with Thai peanut salad	Turkey breast with beet salad (leftover)	Protein pumpkin latté

> Meal planning is a good way to start improving your food choices. It can also decrease the stress of figuring out "what's for dinner" as well as save you time and money.

DAY 1

Day of the Week | Date: _MONDAY, 3/23_   **Time:** _8:30 AM_

STRENGTH TRAINING

FOCUS: CHEST ☐ SHOULDERS ☐ BACK ☐ ARMS ☐ LEGS ☐ CORE ☒ NONE ☐   STRETCH/WARM UP: YES ☒ NO ☐

Exercise/Equipment	SET 1		SET 2		SET 3		SET 4	
	REPS	WEIGHT	REPS	WEIGHT	REPS	WEIGHT	REPS	WEIGHT
CRUNCHES (2 SETS X 10 REPS)	10		10					
CHAIR LEG RAISE (4 SETS X 10-15 REPS)	13		10		10		8	
OBLIQUE LEG RAISE (4 SETS X 10-15 REPS EACH SIDE)	10/10		9/9		8/8		6/6	

> Whether you're doing circuits or strength training, you can use this section to plan your workout and then make a note of the weights you used and the sets and reps you performed.

CARDIO

Exercise / Machine / Class	Duration	Level	Distance	Calories Burned	Heart Rate
TREADMILL INTERVAL WORKOUT	30 MINS	3	—	290	70

OTHER

Exercise / Machine / Class	Duration

NOTES: _TODAY WAS DIFFICULT. MAYBE I SHOULD HAVE A LIGHTER BREAKFAST ON THE DAYS I WORK OUT._

NUTRITION

	Food & Beverage	Calories/ Points	Carbs	Fat	Protein	VIT D
Breakfast TIME: 7:30	BREAKFAST CASSEROLE	197	6	8.3	24.8	400 IU
Snack TIME: 10:20	PUMPKIN-SPICE LATTÉ					
Lunch TIME: 12:45	CHICKEN SKEWERS WITH GREEN SALAD					
Snack TIME: 3:05	PUMPKIN-SPICE LATTÉ	120	4	0	24	
Dinner TIME: 6:35	PORK CHILE VERDE	326	15	5	49	
Snack TIME:						
Total	—	891	35.7	14.3	143.8	400

Write down everything you consume. The more detailed your list, the more accurate your calorie count. All of this information will help you see any weak areas and allow you to make plans to avoid or resist temptation.

DAILY TARGET TOTALS

Cups of Water
☒ ☒ ☒ ☒
☒ ☒ ☒ ☒
☒ ☒ ☒ ☐

Servings of Fruits/ Veggies
☒ ☒ ☒ ☒
☐ ☐ ☐ ☐

Hours of Sleep
☒ ☒ ☒ ☒
☒ ☒ ☐ ☐

RATE HOW CLOSELY YOU MET YOUR GOALS TODAY

☐ ☐ ☐ ☐ ☐ ☐ ☐ ☒ ☐ ☐
10% 20% 30% 40% 50% 60% 70% 80% 90% 100%

NOTES: STAYED UNDER 1200 CALORIES!

SOLID FIRST DAY.

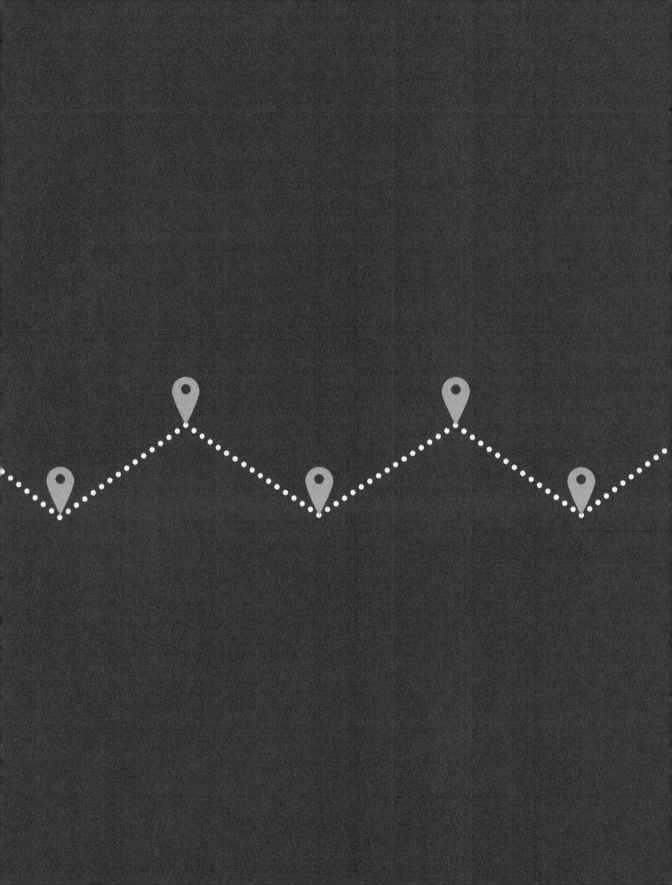

START YOUR
12 WEEKS

GETTING STARTED

Date:

FITNESS

GOAL:

....

....

....

....

....

PLAN:

....

....

....

....

NUTRITION

GOAL:

....

....

....

....

....

PLAN:

....

....

....

....

STARTING STATS

BODY WEIGHT & MEASUREMENTS

	Current	Goal
Weight		
Body Fat %		
Upper Arms		
Chest		
Waist		
Hips		
Thighs		
Calves		

CARDIO

STRENGTH

DAILY TARGETS

Servings of Fruits/Veggies

Calories

Carbs

Fat

Protein

Cups of Water

Hours of Sleep

Other:

Other:

NOTES:

WEEK 1 FITNESS PLAN

Date: _____ to _____

	STRENGTH	CARDIO	CLASS / OTHER
MONDAY			
TUESDAY			
WEDNESDAY			
THURSDAY			
FRIDAY			
SATURDAY			
SUNDAY			

WEEK 1 MEAL PLAN

	BREAKFAST	LUNCH	DINNER	SNACKS
MONDAY				
TUESDAY				
WEDNESDAY				
THURSDAY				
FRIDAY				
SATURDAY				
SUNDAY				

DAY 1

Day of the Week | Date: Time:

STRENGTH TRAINING

FOCUS: CHEST ☐ SHOULDERS ☐ BACK ☐ ARMS ☐ LEGS ☐ CORE ☐ NONE ☐   STRETCH/WARM UP: YES ☐ NO ☐

Exercise/Equipment	SET 1		SET 2		SET 3		SET 4	
	REPS	WEIGHT	REPS	WEIGHT	REPS	WEIGHT	REPS	WEIGHT

CARDIO

Exercise / Machine / Class	Duration	Level	Distance	Calories Burned	Heart Rate

OTHER

Exercise / Machine / Class	Duration

NOTES:

NUTRITION

	Food & Beverage	Calories/Points	Carbs	Fat	Protein	
Breakfast TIME:						
Snack TIME:						
Lunch TIME:						
Snack TIME:						
Dinner TIME:						
Snack TIME:						
Total						

DAILY TARGET TOTALS

Cups of Water ☐☐☐☐☐ ☐☐☐☐☐ ☐☐☐☐☐

Servings of Fruits/ Veggies ☐☐☐☐☐ ☐☐☐☐☐

Hours of Sleep ☐☐☐☐☐ ☐☐☐☐☐

RATE HOW CLOSELY YOU MET YOUR GOALS TODAY

☐ ☐ ☐ ☐ ☐ ☐ ☐ ☐ ☐ ☐
10% 20% 30% 40% 50% 60% 70% 80% 90% 100%

NOTES:

DAY 2

Day of the Week | Date: Time:

STRENGTH TRAINING

FOCUS: CHEST ☐ SHOULDERS ☐ BACK ☐ ARMS ☐ LEGS ☐ CORE ☐ NONE ☐   STRETCH/WARM UP: YES ☐ NO ☐

Exercise/Equipment	SET 1		SET 2		SET 3		SET 4	
	REPS	WEIGHT	REPS	WEIGHT	REPS	WEIGHT	REPS	WEIGHT

CARDIO

Exercise / Machine / Class	Duration	Level	Distance	Calories Burned	Heart Rate

OTHER

Exercise / Machine / Class	Duration

NOTES:

	Food & Beverage	Calories/Points	Carbs	Fat	Protein	
Breakfast TIME:						
Snack TIME:						
Lunch TIME:						
Snack TIME:						
Dinner TIME:						
Snack TIME:						
Total						

DAILY TARGET TOTALS

Cups of Water   ☐ ☐ ☐ ☐ ☐
☐ ☐ ☐ ☐ ☐
☐ ☐ ☐ ☐ ☐

**Servings of Fruits/
Veggies**   ☐ ☐ ☐ ☐ ☐
☐ ☐ ☐ ☐ ☐

Hours of Sleep   ☐ ☐ ☐ ☐ ☐
☐ ☐ ☐ ☐ ☐

RATE HOW CLOSELY YOU MET YOUR GOALS TODAY

☐	☐	☐	☐	☐	☐	☐	☐	☐	☐
10%	20%	30%	40%	50%	60%	70%	80%	90%	100%

NOTES:

....

....

....

DAY 3

Day of the Week | Date: Time:

STRENGTH TRAINING

FOCUS: CHEST ☐ SHOULDERS ☐ BACK ☐ ARMS ☐ LEGS ☐ CORE ☐ NONE ☐   STRETCH/WARM UP: YES ☐ NO ☐

Exercise/Equipment	SET 1		SET 2		SET 3		SET 4	
	REPS	WEIGHT	REPS	WEIGHT	REPS	WEIGHT	REPS	WEIGHT

CARDIO

Exercise / Machine / Class	Duration	Level	Distance	Calories Burned	Heart Rate

OTHER

Exercise / Machine / Class	Duration

NOTES:

NUTRITION

	Food & Beverage	Calories/ Points	Carbs	Fat	Protein	
Breakfast TIME:						
Snack TIME:						
Lunch TIME:						
Snack TIME:						
Dinner TIME:						
Snack TIME:						
Total						

DAILY TARGET TOTALS

Cups of Water	☐ ☐ ☐ ☐ ☐ ☐ ☐ ☐ ☐ ☐ ☐ ☐ ☐ ☐ ☐
Servings of Fruits/ Veggies	☐ ☐ ☐ ☐ ☐ ☐ ☐ ☐ ☐ ☐
Hours of Sleep	☐ ☐ ☐ ☐ ☐ ☐ ☐ ☐ ☐ ☐

RATE HOW CLOSELY YOU MET YOUR GOALS TODAY

☐	☐	☐	☐	☐	☐	☐	☐	☐	☐
10%	20%	30%	40%	50%	60%	70%	80%	90%	100%

NOTES:

DAY 4

Day of the Week | Date: Time:

STRENGTH TRAINING

FOCUS: CHEST ☐ SHOULDERS ☐ BACK ☐ ARMS ☐ LEGS ☐ CORE ☐ NONE ☐   STRETCH/WARM UP: YES ☐ NO ☐

Exercise/Equipment	SET 1		SET 2		SET 3		SET 4	
	REPS	WEIGHT	REPS	WEIGHT	REPS	WEIGHT	REPS	WEIGHT

CARDIO

Exercise / Machine / Class	Duration	Level	Distance	Calories Burned	Heart Rate

OTHER

Exercise / Machine / Class	Duration

NOTES:

NUTRITION

	Food & Beverage	Calories/ Points	Carbs	Fat	Protein	
Breakfast TIME:						
Snack TIME:						
Lunch TIME:						
Snack TIME:						
Dinner TIME:						
Snack TIME:						
Total						

DAILY TARGET TOTALS

Cups of Water ☐☐☐☐☐ ☐☐☐☐☐ ☐☐☐☐☐

Servings of Fruits/ Veggies ☐☐☐☐☐ ☐☐☐☐☐

Hours of Sleep ☐☐☐☐☐ ☐☐☐☐☐

RATE HOW CLOSELY YOU MET YOUR GOALS TODAY

☐ ☐ ☐ ☐ ☐ ☐ ☐ ☐ ☐ ☐
10% 20% 30% 40% 50% 60% 70% 80% 90% 100%

NOTES:

DAY 5

Day of the Week | Date: Time:

STRENGTH TRAINING

FOCUS: CHEST ☐ SHOULDERS ☐ BACK ☐ ARMS ☐ LEGS ☐ CORE ☐ NONE ☐   STRETCH/WARM UP: YES ☐ NO ☐

Exercise/Equipment	SET 1		SET 2		SET 3		SET 4	
	REPS	WEIGHT	REPS	WEIGHT	REPS	WEIGHT	REPS	WEIGHT

CARDIO

Exercise / Machine / Class	Duration	Level	Distance	Calories Burned	Heart Rate

OTHER

Exercise / Machine / Class	Duration

NOTES:

NUTRITION

	Food & Beverage	Calories/ Points	Carbs	Fat	Protein	
Breakfast TIME:						
Snack TIME:						
Lunch TIME:						
Snack TIME:						
Dinner TIME:						
Snack TIME:						
Total						

DAILY TARGET TOTALS

Cups of Water
☐ ☐ ☐ ☐ ☐
☐ ☐ ☐ ☐ ☐
☐ ☐ ☐ ☐ ☐

Servings of Fruits/ Veggies
☐ ☐ ☐ ☐ ☐
☐ ☐ ☐ ☐ ☐

Hours of Sleep
☐ ☐ ☐ ☐ ☐
☐ ☐ ☐ ☐ ☐

RATE HOW CLOSELY YOU MET YOUR GOALS TODAY

☐ ☐ ☐ ☐ ☐ ☐ ☐ ☐ ☐ ☐
10% 20% 30% 40% 50% 60% 70% 80% 90% 100%

NOTES:

DAY 6

Day of the Week | Date: Time:

STRENGTH TRAINING

FOCUS: CHEST ☐ SHOULDERS ☐ BACK ☐ ARMS ☐ LEGS ☐ CORE ☐ NONE ☐   STRETCH/WARM UP: YES ☐ NO ☐

Exercise/Equipment	SET 1		SET 2		SET 3		SET 4	
	REPS	WEIGHT	REPS	WEIGHT	REPS	WEIGHT	REPS	WEIGHT

CARDIO

Exercise / Machine / Class	Duration	Level	Distance	Calories Burned	Heart Rate

OTHER

Exercise / Machine / Class	Duration

NOTES:

NUTRITION

	Food & Beverage	Calories/ Points	Carbs	Fat	Protein	
Breakfast TIME:						
Snack TIME:						
Lunch TIME:						
Snack TIME:						
Dinner TIME:						
Snack TIME:						
Total						

DAILY TARGET TOTALS

Cups of Water ☐☐☐☐☐ ☐☐☐☐☐ ☐☐☐☐☐

Servings of Fruits/ Veggies ☐☐☐☐☐ ☐☐☐☐☐

Hours of Sleep ☐☐☐☐☐ ☐☐☐☐☐

RATE HOW CLOSELY YOU MET YOUR GOALS TODAY

☐	☐	☐	☐	☐	☐	☐	☐	☐	☐
10%	20%	30%	40%	50%	60%	70%	80%	90%	100%

NOTES:

DAY 7

Day of the Week | Date: Time:

STRENGTH TRAINING

FOCUS: CHEST ☐ SHOULDERS ☐ BACK ☐ ARMS ☐ LEGS ☐ CORE ☐ NONE ☐ STRETCH/WARM UP: YES ☐ NO ☐

Exercise/Equipment	SET 1		SET 2		SET 3		SET 4	
	REPS	WEIGHT	REPS	WEIGHT	REPS	WEIGHT	REPS	WEIGHT

CARDIO

Exercise / Machine / Class	Duration	Level	Distance	Calories Burned	Heart Rate

OTHER

Exercise / Machine / Class	Duration

NOTES:

NUTRITION

	Food & Beverage	Calories/ Points	Carbs	Fat	Protein	
Breakfast TIME:						
Snack TIME:						
Lunch TIME:						
Snack TIME:						
Dinner TIME:						
Snack TIME:						
Total						

DAILY TARGET TOTALS

Cups of Water ☐☐☐☐☐ ☐☐☐☐☐ ☐☐☐☐☐

Servings of Fruits/ Veggies ☐☐☐☐☐ ☐☐☐☐☐

Hours of Sleep ☐☐☐☐☐ ☐☐☐☐☐

RATE HOW CLOSELY YOU MET YOUR GOALS TODAY

☐ ☐ ☐ ☐ ☐ ☐ ☐ ☐ ☐ ☐
10% 20% 30% 40% 50% 60% 70% 80% 90% 100%

NOTES:

WEEK 2 FITNESS PLAN

Date: to

	STRENGTH	CARDIO	CLASS / OTHER
MONDAY			
TUESDAY			
WEDNESDAY			
THURSDAY			
FRIDAY			
SATURDAY			
SUNDAY			

WEEK 2 MEAL PLAN

	BREAKFAST	LUNCH	DINNER	SNACKS
MONDAY				
TUESDAY				
WEDNESDAY				
THURSDAY				
FRIDAY				
SATURDAY				
SUNDAY				

DAY 8

Day of the Week | Date: Time:

STRENGTH TRAINING

FOCUS: CHEST ☐ SHOULDERS ☐ BACK ☐ ARMS ☐ LEGS ☐ CORE ☐ NONE ☐   STRETCH/WARM UP: YES ☐ NO ☐

Exercise/Equipment	SET 1		SET 2		SET 3		SET 4	
	REPS	WEIGHT	REPS	WEIGHT	REPS	WEIGHT	REPS	WEIGHT

CARDIO

Exercise / Machine / Class	Duration	Level	Distance	Calories Burned	Heart Rate

OTHER

Exercise / Machine / Class	Duration

NOTES:

NUTRITION

	Food & Beverage	Calories/ Points	Carbs	Fat	Protein	
Breakfast TIME:						
Snack TIME:						
Lunch TIME:						
Snack TIME:						
Dinner TIME:						
Snack TIME:						
Total						

DAILY TARGET TOTALS

Cups of Water ☐☐☐☐☐ ☐☐☐☐☐ ☐☐☐☐☐

Servings of Fruits/ Veggies ☐☐☐☐☐ ☐☐☐☐☐

Hours of Sleep ☐☐☐☐☐ ☐☐☐☐☐

RATE HOW CLOSELY YOU MET YOUR GOALS TODAY

☐ ☐ ☐ ☐ ☐ ☐ ☐ ☐ ☐ ☐
10% 20% 30% 40% 50% 60% 70% 80% 90% 100%

NOTES:

DAY 9

Day of the Week | Date: **Time:**

STRENGTH TRAINING

FOCUS: CHEST ☐ SHOULDERS ☐ BACK ☐ ARMS ☐ LEGS ☐ CORE ☐ NONE ☐   STRETCH/WARM UP: YES ☐ NO ☐

Exercise/Equipment	SET 1		SET 2		SET 3		SET 4	
	REPS	WEIGHT	REPS	WEIGHT	REPS	WEIGHT	REPS	WEIGHT

CARDIO

Exercise / Machine / Class	Duration	Level	Distance	Calories Burned	Heart Rate

OTHER

Exercise / Machine / Class	Duration

NOTES:

NUTRITION

	Food & Beverage	Calories/ Points	Carbs	Fat	Protein	
Breakfast TIME:						
Snack TIME:						
Lunch TIME:						
Snack TIME:						
Dinner TIME:						
Snack TIME:						
Total						

DAILY TARGET TOTALS

Cups of Water	☐ ☐ ☐ ☐ ☐ ☐ ☐ ☐ ☐ ☐ ☐ ☐ ☐ ☐ ☐
Servings of Fruits/ Veggies	☐ ☐ ☐ ☐ ☐ ☐ ☐ ☐ ☐ ☐
Hours of Sleep	☐ ☐ ☐ ☐ ☐ ☐ ☐ ☐ ☐ ☐

RATE HOW CLOSELY YOU MET YOUR GOALS TODAY

☐	☐	☐	☐	☐	☐	☐	☐	☐	☐
10%	20%	30%	40%	50%	60%	70%	80%	90%	100%

NOTES:

DAY 10

Day of the Week | Date: Time:

STRENGTH TRAINING

FOCUS: CHEST ☐ SHOULDERS ☐ BACK ☐ ARMS ☐ LEGS ☐ CORE ☐ NONE ☐   STRETCH/WARM UP: YES ☐ NO ☐

Exercise/Equipment	SET 1		SET 2		SET 3		SET 4	
	REPS	WEIGHT	REPS	WEIGHT	REPS	WEIGHT	REPS	WEIGHT

CARDIO

Exercise / Machine / Class	Duration	Level	Distance	Calories Burned	Heart Rate

OTHER

Exercise / Machine / Class	Duration

NOTES:

NUTRITION

	Food & Beverage	Calories/ Points	Carbs	Fat	Protein	
Breakfast TIME:						
Snack TIME:						
Lunch TIME:						
Snack TIME:						
Dinner TIME:						
Snack TIME:						
Total						

DAILY TARGET TOTALS

Cups of Water ☐☐☐☐☐ ☐☐☐☐☐ ☐☐☐☐☐

Servings of Fruits/ Veggies ☐☐☐☐☐ ☐☐☐☐☐

Hours of Sleep ☐☐☐☐☐ ☐☐☐☐☐

RATE HOW CLOSELY YOU MET YOUR GOALS TODAY

☐ ☐ ☐ ☐ ☐ ☐ ☐ ☐ ☐ ☐
10% 20% 30% 40% 50% 60% 70% 80% 90% 100%

NOTES:

DAY 11

Day of the Week | Date: _____   **Time:** _____

STRENGTH TRAINING

FOCUS: CHEST ☐ SHOULDERS ☐ BACK ☐ ARMS ☐ LEGS ☐ CORE ☐ NONE ☐   STRETCH/WARM UP: YES ☐ NO ☐

Exercise/Equipment	SET 1		SET 2		SET 3		SET 4	
	REPS	WEIGHT	REPS	WEIGHT	REPS	WEIGHT	REPS	WEIGHT

CARDIO

Exercise / Machine / Class	Duration	Level	Distance	Calories Burned	Heart Rate

OTHER

Exercise / Machine / Class	Duration

NOTES:

_____

_____

_____

_____

NUTRITION

	Food & Beverage	Calories/Points	Carbs	Fat	Protein	
Breakfast TIME:						
Snack TIME:						
Lunch TIME:						
Snack TIME:						
Dinner TIME:						
Snack TIME:						
Total						

DAILY TARGET TOTALS

Cups of Water ☐☐☐☐☐ ☐☐☐☐☐ ☐☐☐☐☐

Servings of Fruits/ Veggies ☐☐☐☐☐ ☐☐☐☐☐

Hours of Sleep ☐☐☐☐☐ ☐☐☐☐☐

RATE HOW CLOSELY YOU MET YOUR GOALS TODAY

☐	☐	☐	☐	☐	☐	☐	☐	☐	☐
10%	20%	30%	40%	50%	60%	70%	80%	90%	100%

NOTES:

DAY 12

Day of the Week | Date: Time:

STRENGTH TRAINING

FOCUS: CHEST ☐ SHOULDERS ☐ BACK ☐ ARMS ☐ LEGS ☐ CORE ☐ NONE ☐   STRETCH/WARM UP: YES ☐ NO ☐

Exercise/Equipment	SET 1		SET 2		SET 3		SET 4	
	REPS	WEIGHT	REPS	WEIGHT	REPS	WEIGHT	REPS	WEIGHT

CARDIO

Exercise / Machine / Class	Duration	Level	Distance	Calories Burned	Heart Rate

OTHER

Exercise / Machine / Class	Duration

NOTES:

	Food & Beverage	Calories/ Points	Carbs	Fat	Protein	
Breakfast TIME:						
Snack TIME:						
Lunch TIME:						
Snack TIME:						
Dinner TIME:						
Snack TIME:						
Total						

DAILY TARGET TOTALS

Cups of Water ☐ ☐ ☐ ☐ ☐ ☐ ☐ ☐ ☐ ☐ ☐ ☐ ☐ ☐ ☐

Servings of Fruits/ Veggies ☐ ☐ ☐ ☐ ☐ ☐ ☐ ☐ ☐ ☐

Hours of Sleep ☐ ☐ ☐ ☐ ☐ ☐ ☐ ☐ ☐ ☐

RATE HOW CLOSELY YOU MET YOUR GOALS TODAY

☐ ☐ ☐ ☐ ☐ ☐ ☐ ☐ ☐ ☐
10% 20% 30% 40% 50% 60% 70% 80% 90% 100%

NOTES:

DAY 13

Day of the Week | Date: Time:

STRENGTH TRAINING

FOCUS: CHEST ☐ SHOULDERS ☐ BACK ☐ ARMS ☐ LEGS ☐ CORE ☐ NONE ☐   STRETCH/WARM UP: YES ☐   NO ☐

Exercise/Equipment	SET 1		SET 2		SET 3		SET 4	
	REPS	WEIGHT	REPS	WEIGHT	REPS	WEIGHT	REPS	WEIGHT

CARDIO

Exercise / Machine / Class	Duration	Level	Distance	Calories Burned	Heart Rate

OTHER

Exercise / Machine / Class	Duration

NOTES:

NUTRITION

	Food & Beverage	Calories/ Points	Carbs	Fat	Protein	
Breakfast TIME:						
Snack TIME:						
Lunch TIME:						
Snack TIME:						
Dinner TIME:						
Snack TIME:						
Total						

DAILY TARGET TOTALS

Cups of Water ☐☐☐☐☐ ☐☐☐☐☐ ☐☐☐☐☐

Servings of Fruits/ Veggies ☐☐☐☐☐ ☐☐☐☐☐

Hours of Sleep ☐☐☐☐☐ ☐☐☐☐☐

RATE HOW CLOSELY YOU MET YOUR GOALS TODAY

☐ ☐ ☐ ☐ ☐ ☐ ☐ ☐ ☐ ☐
10% 20% 30% 40% 50% 60% 70% 80% 90% 100%

NOTES:

DAY 14

Day of the Week | Date: Time:

STRENGTH TRAINING

FOCUS: CHEST ☐ SHOULDERS ☐ BACK ☐ ARMS ☐ LEGS ☐ CORE ☐ NONE ☐   STRETCH/WARM UP: YES ☐ NO ☐

Exercise/Equipment	SET 1		SET 2		SET 3		SET 4	
	REPS	WEIGHT	REPS	WEIGHT	REPS	WEIGHT	REPS	WEIGHT

CARDIO

Exercise / Machine / Class	Duration	Level	Distance	Calories Burned	Heart Rate

OTHER

Exercise / Machine / Class	Duration

NOTES:

NUTRITION

	Food & Beverage	Calories/ Points	Carbs	Fat	Protein	
Breakfast TIME:						
Snack TIME:						
Lunch TIME:						
Snack TIME:						
Dinner TIME:						
Snack TIME:						
Total						

DAILY TARGET TOTALS

Cups of Water ☐☐☐☐☐ ☐☐☐☐☐ ☐☐☐☐☐

Servings of Fruits/ Veggies ☐☐☐☐☐ ☐☐☐☐☐

Hours of Sleep ☐☐☐☐☐ ☐☐☐☐☐

RATE HOW CLOSELY YOU MET YOUR GOALS TODAY

☐ ☐ ☐ ☐ ☐ ☐ ☐ ☐ ☐ ☐
10% 20% 30% 40% 50% 60% 70% 80% 90% 100%

NOTES:

WEEK 3 FITNESS PLAN

Dates: _____ to _____

	STRENGTH	CARDIO	CLASS / OTHER
MONDAY			
TUESDAY			
WEDNESDAY			
THURSDAY			
FRIDAY			
SATURDAY			
SUNDAY			

WEEK 3 MEAL PLAN

	BREAKFAST	LUNCH	DINNER	SNACKS
MONDAY				
TUESDAY				
WEDNESDAY				
THURSDAY				
FRIDAY				
SATURDAY				
SUNDAY				

DAY 15

Day of the Week | Date: _____   Time: _____

STRENGTH TRAINING

FOCUS: CHEST ☐ SHOULDERS ☐ BACK ☐ ARMS ☐ LEGS ☐ CORE ☐ NONE ☐   STRETCH/WARM UP: YES ☐ NO ☐

Exercise/Equipment	SET 1		SET 2		SET 3		SET 4	
	REPS	WEIGHT	REPS	WEIGHT	REPS	WEIGHT	REPS	WEIGHT

CARDIO

Exercise / Machine / Class	Duration	Level	Distance	Calories Burned	Heart Rate

OTHER

Exercise / Machine / Class	Duration

NOTES:

NUTRITION

	Food & Beverage	Calories/Points	Carbs	Fat	Protein	
Breakfast TIME:						
Snack TIME:						
Lunch TIME:						
Snack TIME:						
Dinner TIME:						
Snack TIME:						
Total						

DAILY TARGET TOTALS

Cups of Water ☐ ☐ ☐ ☐ ☐ ☐ ☐ ☐ ☐ ☐ ☐ ☐ ☐ ☐ ☐

Servings of Fruits/Veggies ☐ ☐ ☐ ☐ ☐ ☐ ☐ ☐ ☐ ☐

Hours of Sleep ☐ ☐ ☐ ☐ ☐ ☐ ☐ ☐ ☐ ☐

RATE HOW CLOSELY YOU MET YOUR GOALS TODAY

☐	☐	☐	☐	☐	☐	☐	☐	☐	☐
10%	20%	30%	40%	50%	60%	70%	80%	90%	100%

NOTES:

DAY 16

Day of the Week | Date: Time:

STRENGTH TRAINING

FOCUS: CHEST ☐ SHOULDERS ☐ BACK ☐ ARMS ☐ LEGS ☐ CORE ☐ NONE ☐   STRETCH/WARM UP: YES ☐ NO ☐

Exercise/Equipment	SET 1		SET 2		SET 3		SET 4	
	REPS	WEIGHT	REPS	WEIGHT	REPS	WEIGHT	REPS	WEIGHT

CARDIO

Exercise / Machine / Class	Duration	Level	Distance	Calories Burned	Heart Rate

OTHER

Exercise / Machine / Class	Duration

NOTES:

NUTRITION

	Food & Beverage	Calories/Points	Carbs	Fat	Protein	
Breakfast TIME:						
Snack TIME:						
Lunch TIME:						
Snack TIME:						
Dinner TIME:						
Snack TIME:						
Total						

DAILY TARGET TOTALS

Cups of Water
☐ ☐ ☐ ☐ ☐
☐ ☐ ☐ ☐ ☐
☐ ☐ ☐ ☐ ☐

Servings of Fruits/ Veggies
☐ ☐ ☐ ☐ ☐
☐ ☐ ☐ ☐ ☐

Hours of Sleep
☐ ☐ ☐ ☐ ☐
☐ ☐ ☐ ☐ ☐

RATE HOW CLOSELY YOU MET YOUR GOALS TODAY

☐ ☐ ☐ ☐ ☐ ☐ ☐ ☐ ☐ ☐
10% 20% 30% 40% 50% 60% 70% 80% 90% 100%

NOTES:

_____

_____

_____

DAY 17

Day of the Week | Date: Time:

STRENGTH TRAINING

FOCUS: CHEST ☐ SHOULDERS ☐ BACK ☐ ARMS ☐ LEGS ☐ CORE ☐ NONE ☐   STRETCH/WARM UP: YES ☐ NO ☐

Exercise/Equipment	SET 1		SET 2		SET 3		SET 4	
	REPS	WEIGHT	REPS	WEIGHT	REPS	WEIGHT	REPS	WEIGHT

CARDIO

Exercise / Machine / Class	Duration	Level	Distance	Calories Burned	Heart Rate

OTHER

Exercise / Machine / Class	Duration

NOTES:

NUTRITION

	Food & Beverage	Calories/ Points	Carbs	Fat	Protein	
Breakfast TIME:						
Snack TIME:						
Lunch TIME:						
Snack TIME:						
Dinner TIME:						
Snack TIME:						
Total						

DAILY TARGET TOTALS

Cups of Water ☐ ☐ ☐ ☐ ☐ ☐ ☐ ☐ ☐ ☐ ☐ ☐ ☐ ☐ ☐

Servings of Fruits/ Veggies ☐ ☐ ☐ ☐ ☐ ☐ ☐ ☐ ☐ ☐

Hours of Sleep ☐ ☐ ☐ ☐ ☐ ☐ ☐ ☐ ☐ ☐

RATE HOW CLOSELY YOU MET YOUR GOALS TODAY

☐	☐	☐	☐	☐	☐	☐	☐	☐	☐
10%	20%	30%	40%	50%	60%	70%	80%	90%	100%

NOTES:

_____

_____

DAY 18

Day of the Week | Date: Time:

STRENGTH TRAINING

FOCUS: CHEST ☐ SHOULDERS ☐ BACK ☐ ARMS ☐ LEGS ☐ CORE ☐ NONE ☐   STRETCH/WARM UP: YES ☐ NO ☐

Exercise/Equipment	SET 1		SET 2		SET 3		SET 4	
	REPS	WEIGHT	REPS	WEIGHT	REPS	WEIGHT	REPS	WEIGHT

CARDIO

Exercise / Machine / Class	Duration	Level	Distance	Calories Burned	Heart Rate

OTHER

Exercise / Machine / Class	Duration

NOTES:

NUTRITION

	Food & Beverage	Calories/ Points	Carbs	Fat	Protein	
Breakfast TIME:						
Snack TIME:						
Lunch TIME:						
Snack TIME:						
Dinner TIME:						
Snack TIME:						
Total						

DAILY TARGET TOTALS

Cups of Water ☐☐☐☐☐ ☐☐☐☐☐ ☐☐☐☐☐

Servings of Fruits/ Veggies ☐☐☐☐☐ ☐☐☐☐☐

Hours of Sleep ☐☐☐☐☐ ☐☐☐☐☐

RATE HOW CLOSELY YOU MET YOUR GOALS TODAY

☐ ☐ ☐ ☐ ☐ ☐ ☐ ☐ ☐ ☐
10% 20% 30% 40% 50% 60% 70% 80% 90% 100%

NOTES:

DAY 19

Day of the Week | Date: Time:

STRENGTH TRAINING

FOCUS: CHEST ☐ SHOULDERS ☐ BACK ☐ ARMS ☐ LEGS ☐ CORE ☐ NONE ☐   STRETCH/WARM UP: YES ☐ NO ☐

Exercise/Equipment	SET 1		SET 2		SET 3		SET 4	
	REPS	WEIGHT	REPS	WEIGHT	REPS	WEIGHT	REPS	WEIGHT

CARDIO

Exercise / Machine / Class	Duration	Level	Distance	Calories Burned	Heart Rate

OTHER

Exercise / Machine / Class	Duration

NOTES:

NUTRITION

	Food & Beverage	Calories/ Points	Carbs	Fat	Protein	
Breakfast TIME:						
Snack TIME:						
Lunch TIME:						
Snack TIME:						
Dinner TIME:						
Snack TIME:						
Total						

DAILY TARGET TOTALS

Cups of Water ☐☐☐☐☐ ☐☐☐☐☐ ☐☐☐☐☐

Servings of Fruits/ Veggies ☐☐☐☐☐ ☐☐☐☐☐

Hours of Sleep ☐☐☐☐☐ ☐☐☐☐☐

RATE HOW CLOSELY YOU MET YOUR GOALS TODAY

☐	☐	☐	☐	☐	☐	☐	☐	☐	☐
10%	20%	30%	40%	50%	60%	70%	80%	90%	100%

NOTES:

DAY 20

Day of the Week | Date: Time:

STRENGTH TRAINING

FOCUS: CHEST ☐ SHOULDERS ☐ BACK ☐ ARMS ☐ LEGS ☐ CORE ☐ NONE ☐   STRETCH/WARM UP: YES ☐ NO ☐

Exercise/Equipment	SET 1		SET 2		SET 3		SET 4	
	REPS	WEIGHT	REPS	WEIGHT	REPS	WEIGHT	REPS	WEIGHT

CARDIO

Exercise / Machine / Class	Duration	Level	Distance	Calories Burned	Heart Rate

OTHER

Exercise / Machine / Class	Duration

NOTES:

NUTRITION

	Food & Beverage	Calories/ Points	Carbs	Fat	Protein	
Breakfast TIME:						
Snack TIME:						
Lunch TIME:						
Snack TIME:						
Dinner TIME:						
Snack TIME:						
Total						

DAILY TARGET TOTALS

Cups of Water ☐ ☐ ☐ ☐ ☐ ☐ ☐ ☐ ☐ ☐ ☐ ☐ ☐ ☐ ☐

Servings of Fruits/ Veggies ☐ ☐ ☐ ☐ ☐ ☐ ☐ ☐ ☐ ☐

Hours of Sleep ☐ ☐ ☐ ☐ ☐ ☐ ☐ ☐ ☐ ☐

RATE HOW CLOSELY YOU MET YOUR GOALS TODAY

☐ ☐ ☐ ☐ ☐ ☐ ☐ ☐ ☐ ☐
10% 20% 30% 40% 50% 60% 70% 80% 90% 100%

NOTES:

DAY 21

Day of the Week | Date: Time:

STRENGTH TRAINING

FOCUS: CHEST ☐ SHOULDERS ☐ BACK ☐ ARMS ☐ LEGS ☐ CORE ☐ NONE ☐   STRETCH/WARM UP: YES ☐ NO ☐

Exercise/Equipment	SET 1		SET 2		SET 3		SET 4	
	REPS	WEIGHT	REPS	WEIGHT	REPS	WEIGHT	REPS	WEIGHT

CARDIO

Exercise / Machine / Class	Duration	Level	Distance	Calories Burned	Heart Rate

OTHER

Exercise / Machine / Class	Duration

NOTES:

NUTRITION

	Food & Beverage	Calories/Points	Carbs	Fat	Protein	
Breakfast TIME:						
Snack TIME:						
Lunch TIME:						
Snack TIME:						
Dinner TIME:						
Snack TIME:						
Total						

DAILY TARGET TOTALS

Cups of Water ☐ ☐ ☐ ☐ ☐ ☐ ☐ ☐ ☐ ☐ ☐ ☐ ☐ ☐ ☐

Servings of Fruits/Veggies ☐ ☐ ☐ ☐ ☐ ☐ ☐ ☐ ☐ ☐

Hours of Sleep ☐ ☐ ☐ ☐ ☐ ☐ ☐ ☐ ☐ ☐

RATE HOW CLOSELY YOU MET YOUR GOALS TODAY

☐ ☐ ☐ ☐ ☐ ☐ ☐ ☐ ☐ ☐
10% 20% 30% 40% 50% 60% 70% 80% 90% 100%

NOTES:

WEEK 4 FITNESS PLAN

Dates: _____ to _____

	STRENGTH	CARDIO	CLASS / OTHER
MONDAY			
TUESDAY			
WEDNESDAY			
THURSDAY			
FRIDAY			
SATURDAY			
SUNDAY			

WEEK 4 MEAL PLAN

	BREAKFAST	LUNCH	DINNER	SNACKS
MONDAY				
TUESDAY				
WEDNESDAY				
THURSDAY				
FRIDAY				
SATURDAY				
SUNDAY				

DAY 22

Day of the Week | Date: Time:

STRENGTH TRAINING

FOCUS: CHEST ☐ SHOULDERS ☐ BACK ☐ ARMS ☐ LEGS ☐ CORE ☐ NONE ☐   STRETCH/WARM UP: YES ☐ NO ☐

Exercise/Equipment	SET 1		SET 2		SET 3		SET 4	
	REPS	WEIGHT	REPS	WEIGHT	REPS	WEIGHT	REPS	WEIGHT

CARDIO

Exercise / Machine / Class	Duration	Level	Distance	Calories Burned	Heart Rate

OTHER

Exercise / Machine / Class	Duration

NOTES:

	Food & Beverage	Calories/ Points	Carbs	Fat	Protein	
Breakfast TIME:						
Snack TIME:						
Lunch TIME:						
Snack TIME:						
Dinner TIME:						
Snack TIME:						
Total						

DAILY TARGET TOTALS

Cups of Water
☐ ☐ ☐ ☐ ☐
☐ ☐ ☐ ☐ ☐
☐ ☐ ☐ ☐ ☐

Servings of Fruits/ Veggies
☐ ☐ ☐ ☐ ☐
☐ ☐ ☐ ☐ ☐

Hours of Sleep
☐ ☐ ☐ ☐ ☐
☐ ☐ ☐ ☐ ☐

RATE HOW CLOSELY YOU MET YOUR GOALS TODAY

☐ ☐ ☐ ☐ ☐ ☐ ☐ ☐ ☐ ☐
10% 20% 30% 40% 50% 60% 70% 80% 90% 100%

NOTES:

DAY 23

Day of the Week | Date: **Time:**

STRENGTH TRAINING

FOCUS: CHEST ☐ SHOULDERS ☐ BACK ☐ ARMS ☐ LEGS ☐ CORE ☐ NONE ☐   STRETCH/WARM UP: YES ☐ NO ☐

Exercise/Equipment	SET 1		SET 2		SET 3		SET 4	
	REPS	WEIGHT	REPS	WEIGHT	REPS	WEIGHT	REPS	WEIGHT

CARDIO

Exercise / Machine / Class	Duration	Level	Distance	Calories Burned	Heart Rate

OTHER

Exercise / Machine / Class	Duration

NOTES:

NUTRITION

	Food & Beverage	Calories/Points	Carbs	Fat	Protein	
Breakfast TIME:						
Snack TIME:						
Lunch TIME:						
Snack TIME:						
Dinner TIME:						
Snack TIME:						
Total						

DAILY TARGET TOTALS

Cups of Water ☐ ☐ ☐ ☐ ☐ ☐ ☐ ☐ ☐ ☐ ☐ ☐ ☐ ☐ ☐

Servings of Fruits/ Veggies ☐ ☐ ☐ ☐ ☐ ☐ ☐ ☐ ☐ ☐

Hours of Sleep ☐ ☐ ☐ ☐ ☐ ☐ ☐ ☐ ☐ ☐

RATE HOW CLOSELY YOU MET YOUR GOALS TODAY

☐ ☐ ☐ ☐ ☐ ☐ ☐ ☐ ☐ ☐

10% 20% 30% 40% 50% 60% 70% 80% 90% 100%

NOTES:

DAY 24

Day of the Week | Date: Time:

STRENGTH TRAINING

FOCUS: CHEST ☐ SHOULDERS ☐ BACK ☐ ARMS ☐ LEGS ☐ CORE ☐ NONE ☐   STRETCH/WARM UP: YES ☐ NO ☐

Exercise/Equipment	SET 1		SET 2		SET 3		SET 4	
	REPS	WEIGHT	REPS	WEIGHT	REPS	WEIGHT	REPS	WEIGHT

CARDIO

Exercise / Machine / Class	Duration	Level	Distance	Calories Burned	Heart Rate

OTHER

Exercise / Machine / Class	Duration

NOTES:

NUTRITION

	Food & Beverage	Calories/ Points	Carbs	Fat	Protein	
Breakfast TIME:						
Snack TIME:						
Lunch TIME:						
Snack TIME:						
Dinner TIME:						
Snack TIME:						
Total						

DAILY TARGET TOTALS

Cups of Water ☐☐☐☐☐ ☐☐☐☐☐ ☐☐☐☐☐

Servings of Fruits/ Veggies ☐☐☐☐☐ ☐☐☐☐☐

Hours of Sleep ☐☐☐☐☐ ☐☐☐☐☐

RATE HOW CLOSELY YOU MET YOUR GOALS TODAY

☐	☐	☐	☐	☐	☐	☐	☐	☐	☐
10%	20%	30%	40%	50%	60%	70%	80%	90%	100%

NOTES:

_____

_____

_____

DAY 25

Day of the Week | Date: Time:

STRENGTH TRAINING

FOCUS: CHEST ☐ SHOULDERS ☐ BACK ☐ ARMS ☐ LEGS ☐ CORE ☐ NONE ☐   STRETCH/WARM UP: YES ☐ NO ☐

Exercise/Equipment	SET 1		SET 2		SET 3		SET 4	
	REPS	WEIGHT	REPS	WEIGHT	REPS	WEIGHT	REPS	WEIGHT

CARDIO

Exercise / Machine / Class	Duration	Level	Distance	Calories Burned	Heart Rate

OTHER

Exercise / Machine / Class	Duration

NOTES:

NUTRITION

	Food & Beverage	Calories/ Points	Carbs	Fat	Protein	
Breakfast TIME:						
Snack TIME:						
Lunch TIME:						
Snack TIME:						
Dinner TIME:						
Snack TIME:						
Total						

DAILY TARGET TOTALS

Cups of Water ☐☐☐☐☐ ☐☐☐☐☐ ☐☐☐☐☐

Servings of Fruits/ Veggies ☐☐☐☐☐ ☐☐☐☐☐

Hours of Sleep ☐☐☐☐☐ ☐☐☐☐☐

RATE HOW CLOSELY YOU MET YOUR GOALS TODAY

☐	☐	☐	☐	☐	☐	☐	☐	☐	☐
10%	20%	30%	40%	50%	60%	70%	80%	90%	100%

NOTES:

DAY 26

Day of the Week | Date: Time:

STRENGTH TRAINING

FOCUS: CHEST ☐ SHOULDERS ☐ BACK ☐ ARMS ☐ LEGS ☐ CORE ☐ NONE ☐   STRETCH/WARM UP: YES ☐ NO ☐

Exercise/Equipment	SET 1		SET 2		SET 3		SET 4	
	REPS	WEIGHT	REPS	WEIGHT	REPS	WEIGHT	REPS	WEIGHT

CARDIO

Exercise / Machine / Class	Duration	Level	Distance	Calories Burned	Heart Rate

OTHER

Exercise / Machine / Class	Duration

NOTES:

NUTRITION

	Food & Beverage	Calories/Points	Carbs	Fat	Protein	
Breakfast TIME:						
Snack TIME:						
Lunch TIME:						
Snack TIME:						
Dinner TIME:						
Snack TIME:						
Total						

DAILY TARGET TOTALS

Cups of Water
☐ ☐ ☐ ☐ ☐
☐ ☐ ☐ ☐ ☐
☐ ☐ ☐ ☐ ☐

Servings of Fruits/ Veggies
☐ ☐ ☐ ☐ ☐
☐ ☐ ☐ ☐ ☐

Hours of Sleep
☐ ☐ ☐ ☐ ☐
☐ ☐ ☐ ☐ ☐

RATE HOW CLOSELY YOU MET YOUR GOALS TODAY

☐	☐	☐	☐	☐	☐	☐	☐	☐	☐
10%	20%	30%	40%	50%	60%	70%	80%	90%	100%

NOTES:

_____

_____

_____

DAY 27

Day of the Week | Date: Time:

STRENGTH TRAINING

FOCUS: CHEST ☐ SHOULDERS ☐ BACK ☐ ARMS ☐ LEGS ☐ CORE ☐ NONE ☐   STRETCH/WARM UP: YES ☐ NO ☐

Exercise/Equipment	SET 1		SET 2		SET 3		SET 4	
	REPS	WEIGHT	REPS	WEIGHT	REPS	WEIGHT	REPS	WEIGHT

CARDIO

Exercise / Machine / Class	Duration	Level	Distance	Calories Burned	Heart Rate

OTHER

Exercise / Machine / Class	Duration

NOTES:

NUTRITION

	Food & Beverage	Calories/ Points	Carbs	Fat	Protein	
Breakfast TIME:						
Snack TIME:						
Lunch TIME:						
Snack TIME:						
Dinner TIME:						
Snack TIME:						
Total						

DAILY TARGET TOTALS

Cups of Water ☐☐☐☐☐ ☐☐☐☐☐ ☐☐☐☐☐

Servings of Fruits/ Veggies ☐☐☐☐☐ ☐☐☐☐☐

Hours of Sleep ☐☐☐☐☐ ☐☐☐☐☐

RATE HOW CLOSELY YOU MET YOUR GOALS TODAY

☐ ☐ ☐ ☐ ☐ ☐ ☐ ☐ ☐ ☐
10% 20% 30% 40% 50% 60% 70% 80% 90% 100%

NOTES:

DAY 28

Day of the Week | Date: Time:

STRENGTH TRAINING

FOCUS: CHEST ☐ SHOULDERS ☐ BACK ☐ ARMS ☐ LEGS ☐ CORE ☐ NONE ☐   STRETCH/WARM UP: YES ☐ NO ☐

Exercise/Equipment	SET 1		SET 2		SET 3		SET 4	
	REPS	WEIGHT	REPS	WEIGHT	REPS	WEIGHT	REPS	WEIGHT

CARDIO

Exercise / Machine / Class	Duration	Level	Distance	Calories Burned	Heart Rate

OTHER

Exercise / Machine / Class	Duration

NOTES:

NUTRITION

	Food & Beverage	Calories/ Points	Carbs	Fat	Protein	
Breakfast TIME:						
Snack TIME:						
Lunch TIME:						
Snack TIME:						
Dinner TIME:						
Snack TIME:						
Total						

DAILY TARGET TOTALS

Cups of Water ☐ ☐ ☐ ☐ ☐ ☐ ☐ ☐ ☐ ☐ ☐ ☐ ☐ ☐ ☐

Servings of Fruits/ Veggies ☐ ☐ ☐ ☐ ☐ ☐ ☐ ☐ ☐ ☐

Hours of Sleep ☐ ☐ ☐ ☐ ☐ ☐ ☐ ☐ ☐ ☐

RATE HOW CLOSELY YOU MET YOUR GOALS TODAY

☐ ☐ ☐ ☐ ☐ ☐ ☐ ☐ ☐ ☐
10% 20% 30% 40% 50% 60% 70% 80% 90% 100%

NOTES:

28-DAY CHECK-IN

NOTES

Date:

CURRENT STATS

BODY WEIGHT & MEASUREMENTS

	Current	Goal
Weight		
Body Fat %		
Upper Arms		
Chest		
Waist		
Hips		
Thighs		
Calves		

CARDIO

STRENGTH

ACHIEVING MY GOALS

10%	20%	30%	40%	50%	60%	70%	80%	90%	100%
☐	☐	☐	☐	☐	☐	☐	☐	☐	☐

WEEK 5 FITNESS PLAN

Dates: _____ to _____

	STRENGTH	CARDIO	CLASS / OTHER
MONDAY			
TUESDAY			
WEDNESDAY			
THURSDAY			
FRIDAY			
SATURDAY			
SUNDAY			

WEEK 5 MEAL PLAN

	BREAKFAST	LUNCH	DINNER	SNACKS
MONDAY				
TUESDAY				
WEDNESDAY				
THURSDAY				
FRIDAY				
SATURDAY				
SUNDAY				

DAY 29

Day of the Week | Date: Time:

STRENGTH TRAINING

FOCUS: CHEST ☐ SHOULDERS ☐ BACK ☐ ARMS ☐ LEGS ☐ CORE ☐ NONE ☐   STRETCH/WARM UP: YES ☐ NO ☐

Exercise/Equipment	SET 1		SET 2		SET 3		SET 4	
	REPS	WEIGHT	REPS	WEIGHT	REPS	WEIGHT	REPS	WEIGHT

CARDIO

Exercise / Machine / Class	Duration	Level	Distance	Calories Burned	Heart Rate

OTHER

Exercise / Machine / Class	Duration

NOTES:

NUTRITION

	Food & Beverage	Calories/ Points	Carbs	Fat	Protein	
Breakfast TIME:						
Snack TIME:						
Lunch TIME:						
Snack TIME:						
Dinner TIME:						
Snack TIME:						
Total						

DAILY TARGET TOTALS

Cups of Water
☐ ☐ ☐ ☐ ☐
☐ ☐ ☐ ☐ ☐
☐ ☐ ☐ ☐ ☐

Servings of Fruits/ Veggies
☐ ☐ ☐ ☐ ☐
☐ ☐ ☐ ☐ ☐

Hours of Sleep
☐ ☐ ☐ ☐ ☐
☐ ☐ ☐ ☐ ☐

RATE HOW CLOSELY YOU MET YOUR GOALS TODAY

☐ ☐ ☐ ☐ ☐ ☐ ☐ ☐ ☐ ☐
10% 20% 30% 40% 50% 60% 70% 80% 90% 100%

NOTES:

DAY 30

Day of the Week | Date: Time:

STRENGTH TRAINING

FOCUS: CHEST ☐ SHOULDERS ☐ BACK ☐ ARMS ☐ LEGS ☐ CORE ☐ NONE ☐   STRETCH/WARM UP: YES ☐ NO ☐

Exercise/Equipment	SET 1		SET 2		SET 3		SET 4	
	REPS	WEIGHT	REPS	WEIGHT	REPS	WEIGHT	REPS	WEIGHT

CARDIO

Exercise / Machine / Class	Duration	Level	Distance	Calories Burned	Heart Rate

OTHER

Exercise / Machine / Class	Duration

NOTES:

NUTRITION

	Food & Beverage	Calories/ Points	Carbs	Fat	Protein	
Breakfast TIME:						
Snack TIME:						
Lunch TIME:						
Snack TIME:						
Dinner TIME:						
Snack TIME:						
Total						

DAILY TARGET TOTALS

Cups of Water ☐☐☐☐☐ ☐☐☐☐☐ ☐☐☐☐☐

Servings of Fruits/ Veggies ☐☐☐☐☐ ☐☐☐☐☐

Hours of Sleep ☐☐☐☐☐ ☐☐☐☐☐

RATE HOW CLOSELY YOU MET YOUR GOALS TODAY

☐ ☐ ☐ ☐ ☐ ☐ ☐ ☐ ☐ ☐
10% 20% 30% 40% 50% 60% 70% 80% 90% 100%

NOTES:

DAY 31

Day of the Week | Date: _____   Time: _____

STRENGTH TRAINING

FOCUS: CHEST ☐ SHOULDERS ☐ BACK ☐ ARMS ☐ LEGS ☐ CORE ☐ NONE ☐   STRETCH/WARM UP: YES ☐ NO ☐

Exercise/Equipment	SET 1		SET 2		SET 3		SET 4	
	REPS	WEIGHT	REPS	WEIGHT	REPS	WEIGHT	REPS	WEIGHT

CARDIO

Exercise / Machine / Class	Duration	Level	Distance	Calories Burned	Heart Rate

OTHER

Exercise / Machine / Class	Duration

NOTES:

NUTRITION

	Food & Beverage	Calories/ Points	Carbs	Fat	Protein	
Breakfast TIME:						
Snack TIME:						
Lunch TIME:						
Snack TIME:						
Dinner TIME:						
Snack TIME:						
Total						

DAILY TARGET TOTALS

Cups of Water ☐☐☐☐☐ ☐☐☐☐☐ ☐☐☐☐☐

Servings of Fruits/ Veggies ☐☐☐☐☐ ☐☐☐☐☐

Hours of Sleep ☐☐☐☐☐ ☐☐☐☐☐

RATE HOW CLOSELY YOU MET YOUR GOALS TODAY

☐ ☐ ☐ ☐ ☐ ☐ ☐ ☐ ☐ ☐
10% 20% 30% 40% 50% 60% 70% 80% 90% 100%

NOTES:

DAY 32

Day of the Week | Date: Time:

STRENGTH TRAINING

FOCUS: CHEST ☐ SHOULDERS ☐ BACK ☐ ARMS ☐ LEGS ☐ CORE ☐ NONE ☐   STRETCH/WARM UP: YES ☐ NO ☐

Exercise/Equipment	SET 1		SET 2		SET 3		SET 4	
	REPS	WEIGHT	REPS	WEIGHT	REPS	WEIGHT	REPS	WEIGHT

CARDIO

Exercise / Machine / Class	Duration	Level	Distance	Calories Burned	Heart Rate

OTHER

Exercise / Machine / Class	Duration

NOTES:

NUTRITION

	Food & Beverage	Calories/Points	Carbs	Fat	Protein	
Breakfast TIME:						
Snack TIME:						
Lunch TIME:						
Snack TIME:						
Dinner TIME:						
Snack TIME:						
Total						

DAILY TARGET TOTALS

Cups of Water ☐ ☐ ☐ ☐ ☐ ☐ ☐ ☐ ☐ ☐ ☐ ☐ ☐ ☐ ☐

Servings of Fruits/ Veggies ☐ ☐ ☐ ☐ ☐ ☐ ☐ ☐ ☐ ☐

Hours of Sleep ☐ ☐ ☐ ☐ ☐ ☐ ☐ ☐ ☐ ☐

RATE HOW CLOSELY YOU MET YOUR GOALS TODAY

☐	☐	☐	☐	☐	☐	☐	☐	☐	☐
10%	20%	30%	40%	50%	60%	70%	80%	90%	100%

NOTES:

....

....

....

....

DAY 33

Day of the Week | Date: Time:

STRENGTH TRAINING

FOCUS: CHEST ☐ SHOULDERS ☐ BACK ☐ ARMS ☐ LEGS ☐ CORE ☐ NONE ☐   STRETCH/WARM UP: YES ☐ NO ☐

Exercise/Equipment	SET 1		SET 2		SET 3		SET 4	
	REPS	WEIGHT	REPS	WEIGHT	REPS	WEIGHT	REPS	WEIGHT

CARDIO

Exercise / Machine / Class	Duration	Level	Distance	Calories Burned	Heart Rate

OTHER

Exercise / Machine / Class	Duration

NOTES:

NUTRITION

	Food & Beverage	Calories/ Points	Carbs	Fat	Protein	
Breakfast TIME:						
Snack TIME:						
Lunch TIME:						
Snack TIME:						
Dinner TIME:						
Snack TIME:						
Total						

DAILY TARGET TOTALS

Cups of Water ☐☐☐☐☐ ☐☐☐☐☐ ☐☐☐☐☐

Servings of Fruits/ Veggies ☐☐☐☐☐ ☐☐☐☐☐

Hours of Sleep ☐☐☐☐☐ ☐☐☐☐☐

RATE HOW CLOSELY YOU MET YOUR GOALS TODAY

☐	☐	☐	☐	☐	☐	☐	☐	☐	☐
10%	20%	30%	40%	50%	60%	70%	80%	90%	100%

NOTES:

DAY 34

Day of the Week | Date: Time:

STRENGTH TRAINING

FOCUS: CHEST ☐ SHOULDERS ☐ BACK ☐ ARMS ☐ LEGS ☐ CORE ☐ NONE ☐   STRETCH/WARM UP: YES ☐ NO ☐

Exercise/Equipment	SET 1		SET 2		SET 3		SET 4	
	REPS	WEIGHT	REPS	WEIGHT	REPS	WEIGHT	REPS	WEIGHT

CARDIO

Exercise / Machine / Class	Duration	Level	Distance	Calories Burned	Heart Rate

OTHER

Exercise / Machine / Class	Duration

NOTES:

NUTRITION

	Food & Beverage	Calories/ Points	Carbs	Fat	Protein	
Breakfast TIME:						
Snack TIME:						
Lunch TIME:						
Snack TIME:						
Dinner TIME:						
Snack TIME:						
Total						

DAILY TARGET TOTALS

Cups of Water ☐☐☐☐☐ ☐☐☐☐☐ ☐☐☐☐☐

Servings of Fruits/ Veggies ☐☐☐☐☐ ☐☐☐☐☐

Hours of Sleep ☐☐☐☐☐ ☐☐☐☐☐

RATE HOW CLOSELY YOU MET YOUR GOALS TODAY

☐ ☐ ☐ ☐ ☐ ☐ ☐ ☐ ☐ ☐
10% 20% 30% 40% 50% 60% 70% 80% 90% 100%

NOTES:

_____

_____

_____

_____

DAY 35

Day of the Week | Date: Time:

STRENGTH TRAINING

FOCUS: CHEST ☐ SHOULDERS ☐ BACK ☐ ARMS ☐ LEGS ☐ CORE ☐ NONE ☐   STRETCH/WARM UP: YES ☐ NO ☐

Exercise/Equipment	SET 1		SET 2		SET 3		SET 4	
	REPS	WEIGHT	REPS	WEIGHT	REPS	WEIGHT	REPS	WEIGHT

CARDIO

Exercise / Machine / Class	Duration	Level	Distance	Calories Burned	Heart Rate

OTHER

Exercise / Machine / Class	Duration

NOTES:

NUTRITION

	Food & Beverage	Calories/Points	Carbs	Fat	Protein	
Breakfast TIME:						
Snack TIME:						
Lunch TIME:						
Snack TIME:						
Dinner TIME:						
Snack TIME:						
Total						

DAILY TARGET TOTALS

Cups of Water ☐☐☐☐☐ ☐☐☐☐☐ ☐☐☐☐☐

Servings of Fruits/ Veggies ☐☐☐☐☐ ☐☐☐☐☐

Hours of Sleep ☐☐☐☐☐ ☐☐☐☐☐

RATE HOW CLOSELY YOU MET YOUR GOALS TODAY

☐ ☐ ☐ ☐ ☐ ☐ ☐ ☐ ☐ ☐
10% 20% 30% 40% 50% 60% 70% 80% 90% 100%

NOTES:

WEEK 6 FITNESS PLAN

Dates: to

	STRENGTH	CARDIO	CLASS / OTHER
MONDAY			
TUESDAY			
WEDNESDAY			
THURSDAY			
FRIDAY			
SATURDAY			
SUNDAY			

WEEK 6 MEAL PLAN

	BREAKFAST	LUNCH	DINNER	SNACKS
MONDAY				
TUESDAY				
WEDNESDAY				
THURSDAY				
FRIDAY				
SATURDAY				
SUNDAY				

DAY 36

Day of the Week | Date: Time:

STRENGTH TRAINING

FOCUS: CHEST ☐ SHOULDERS ☐ BACK ☐ ARMS ☐ LEGS ☐ CORE ☐ NONE ☐   STRETCH/WARM UP: YES ☐   NO ☐

Exercise/Equipment	SET 1		SET 2		SET 3		SET 4	
	REPS	WEIGHT	REPS	WEIGHT	REPS	WEIGHT	REPS	WEIGHT

CARDIO

Exercise / Machine / Class	Duration	Level	Distance	Calories Burned	Heart Rate

OTHER

Exercise / Machine / Class	Duration

NOTES:

NUTRITION

	Food & Beverage	Calories/Points	Carbs	Fat	Protein	
Breakfast TIME:						
Snack TIME:						
Lunch TIME:						
Snack TIME:						
Dinner TIME:						
Snack TIME:						
Total						

DAILY TARGET TOTALS

Cups of Water ☐☐☐☐☐ ☐☐☐☐☐ ☐☐☐☐☐

Servings of Fruits/ Veggies ☐☐☐☐☐ ☐☐☐☐☐

Hours of Sleep ☐☐☐☐☐ ☐☐☐☐☐

RATE HOW CLOSELY YOU MET YOUR GOALS TODAY

☐ ☐ ☐ ☐ ☐ ☐ ☐ ☐ ☐ ☐
10% 20% 30% 40% 50% 60% 70% 80% 90% 100%

NOTES:

DAY 37

Day of the Week | Date: Time:

STRENGTH TRAINING

FOCUS: CHEST ☐ SHOULDERS ☐ BACK ☐ ARMS ☐ LEGS ☐ CORE ☐ NONE ☐   STRETCH/WARM UP: YES ☐ NO ☐

Exercise/Equipment	SET 1		SET 2		SET 3		SET 4	
	REPS	WEIGHT	REPS	WEIGHT	REPS	WEIGHT	REPS	WEIGHT

CARDIO

Exercise / Machine / Class	Duration	Level	Distance	Calories Burned	Heart Rate

OTHER

Exercise / Machine / Class	Duration

NOTES:

NUTRITION

	Food & Beverage	Calories/Points	Carbs	Fat	Protein	
Breakfast TIME:						
Snack TIME:						
Lunch TIME:						
Snack TIME:						
Dinner TIME:						
Snack TIME:						
Total						

DAILY TARGET TOTALS

Cups of Water ☐☐☐☐☐ ☐☐☐☐☐ ☐☐☐☐☐

Servings of Fruits/ Veggies ☐☐☐☐☐ ☐☐☐☐☐

Hours of Sleep ☐☐☐☐☐ ☐☐☐☐☐

RATE HOW CLOSELY YOU MET YOUR GOALS TODAY

☐ ☐ ☐ ☐ ☐ ☐ ☐ ☐ ☐ ☐

10% 20% 30% 40% 50% 60% 70% 80% 90% 100%

NOTES:

DAY 38

Day of the Week | Date: Time:

STRENGTH TRAINING

FOCUS: CHEST ☐ SHOULDERS ☐ BACK ☐ ARMS ☐ LEGS ☐ CORE ☐ NONE ☐   STRETCH/WARM UP: YES ☐ NO ☐

Exercise/Equipment	SET 1		SET 2		SET 3		SET 4	
	REPS	WEIGHT	REPS	WEIGHT	REPS	WEIGHT	REPS	WEIGHT

CARDIO

Exercise / Machine / Class	Duration	Level	Distance	Calories Burned	Heart Rate

OTHER

Exercise / Machine / Class	Duration

NOTES:

NUTRITION

	Food & Beverage	Calories/Points	Carbs	Fat	Protein	
Breakfast TIME:						
Snack TIME:						
Lunch TIME:						
Snack TIME:						
Dinner TIME:						
Snack TIME:						
Total						

DAILY TARGET TOTALS

Cups of Water
☐ ☐ ☐ ☐ ☐
☐ ☐ ☐ ☐ ☐
☐ ☐ ☐ ☐ ☐

Servings of Fruits/ Veggies
☐ ☐ ☐ ☐ ☐
☐ ☐ ☐ ☐ ☐

Hours of Sleep
☐ ☐ ☐ ☐ ☐
☐ ☐ ☐ ☐ ☐

RATE HOW CLOSELY YOU MET YOUR GOALS TODAY

☐ ☐ ☐ ☐ ☐ ☐ ☐ ☐ ☐ ☐
10% 20% 30% 40% 50% 60% 70% 80% 90% 100%

NOTES:

DAY 39

Day of the Week | Date: Time:

STRENGTH TRAINING

FOCUS: CHEST ☐ SHOULDERS ☐ BACK ☐ ARMS ☐ LEGS ☐ CORE ☐ NONE ☐   STRETCH/WARM UP: YES ☐ NO ☐

Exercise/Equipment	SET 1		SET 2		SET 3		SET 4	
	REPS	WEIGHT	REPS	WEIGHT	REPS	WEIGHT	REPS	WEIGHT

CARDIO

Exercise / Machine / Class	Duration	Level	Distance	Calories Burned	Heart Rate

OTHER

Exercise / Machine / Class	Duration

NOTES:

NUTRITION

	Food & Beverage	Calories/ Points	Carbs	Fat	Protein	
Breakfast TIME:						
Snack TIME:						
Lunch TIME:						
Snack TIME:						
Dinner TIME:						
Snack TIME:						
Total						

DAILY TARGET TOTALS

Cups of Water ☐☐☐☐☐ ☐☐☐☐☐ ☐☐☐☐☐

Servings of Fruits/ Veggies ☐☐☐☐☐ ☐☐☐☐☐

Hours of Sleep ☐☐☐☐☐ ☐☐☐☐☐

RATE HOW CLOSELY YOU MET YOUR GOALS TODAY

☐ ☐ ☐ ☐ ☐ ☐ ☐ ☐ ☐ ☐
10% 20% 30% 40% 50% 60% 70% 80% 90% 100%

NOTES:

DAY 40

Day of the Week | Date: Time:

STRENGTH TRAINING

FOCUS: CHEST ☐ SHOULDERS ☐ BACK ☐ ARMS ☐ LEGS ☐ CORE ☐ NONE ☐   STRETCH/WARM UP: YES ☐ NO ☐

Exercise/Equipment	SET 1		SET 2		SET 3		SET 4	
	REPS	WEIGHT	REPS	WEIGHT	REPS	WEIGHT	REPS	WEIGHT

CARDIO

Exercise / Machine / Class	Duration	Level	Distance	Calories Burned	Heart Rate

OTHER

Exercise / Machine / Class	Duration

NOTES:

NUTRITION

	Food & Beverage	Calories/ Points	Carbs	Fat	Protein	
Breakfast TIME:						
Snack TIME:						
Lunch TIME:						
Snack TIME:						
Dinner TIME:						
Snack TIME:						
Total						

DAILY TARGET TOTALS

Cups of Water ☐☐☐☐☐ ☐☐☐☐☐ ☐☐☐☐☐

Servings of Fruits/ Veggies ☐☐☐☐☐ ☐☐☐☐☐

Hours of Sleep ☐☐☐☐☐ ☐☐☐☐☐

RATE HOW CLOSELY YOU MET YOUR GOALS TODAY

☐ ☐ ☐ ☐ ☐ ☐ ☐ ☐ ☐ ☐
10% 20% 30% 40% 50% 60% 70% 80% 90% 100%

NOTES:

DAY 41

Day of the Week | Date: **Time:**

STRENGTH TRAINING

FOCUS: CHEST ☐ SHOULDERS ☐ BACK ☐ ARMS ☐ LEGS ☐ CORE ☐ NONE ☐   STRETCH/WARM UP: YES ☐ NO ☐

Exercise/Equipment	SET 1		SET 2		SET 3		SET 4	
	REPS	WEIGHT	REPS	WEIGHT	REPS	WEIGHT	REPS	WEIGHT

CARDIO

Exercise / Machine / Class	Duration	Level	Distance	Calories Burned	Heart Rate

OTHER

Exercise / Machine / Class	Duration

NOTES:

NUTRITION

	Food & Beverage	Calories/Points	Carbs	Fat	Protein	
Breakfast TIME:						
Snack TIME:						
Lunch TIME:						
Snack TIME:						
Dinner TIME:						
Snack TIME:						
Total						

DAILY TARGET TOTALS

Cups of Water ☐☐☐☐☐ ☐☐☐☐☐ ☐☐☐☐☐

Servings of Fruits/ Veggies ☐☐☐☐☐ ☐☐☐☐☐

Hours of Sleep ☐☐☐☐☐ ☐☐☐☐☐

RATE HOW CLOSELY YOU MET YOUR GOALS TODAY

☐ ☐ ☐ ☐ ☐ ☐ ☐ ☐ ☐ ☐
10% 20% 30% 40% 50% 60% 70% 80% 90% 100%

NOTES:

DAY 42

Day of the Week | Date: Time:

STRENGTH TRAINING

FOCUS: CHEST ☐ SHOULDERS ☐ BACK ☐ ARMS ☐ LEGS ☐ CORE ☐ NONE ☐   STRETCH/WARM UP: YES ☐ NO ☐

Exercise/Equipment	SET 1		SET 2		SET 3		SET 4	
	REPS	WEIGHT	REPS	WEIGHT	REPS	WEIGHT	REPS	WEIGHT

CARDIO

Exercise / Machine / Class	Duration	Level	Distance	Calories Burned	Heart Rate

OTHER

Exercise / Machine / Class	Duration

NOTES:

NUTRITION

	Food & Beverage	Calories/ Points	Carbs	Fat	Protein	
Breakfast TIME:						
Snack TIME:						
Lunch TIME:						
Snack TIME:						
Dinner TIME:						
Snack TIME:						
Total						

DAILY TARGET TOTALS

Cups of Water ☐ ☐ ☐ ☐ ☐
☐ ☐ ☐ ☐ ☐
☐ ☐ ☐ ☐ ☐

Servings of Fruits/ Veggies ☐ ☐ ☐ ☐ ☐
☐ ☐ ☐ ☐ ☐

Hours of Sleep ☐ ☐ ☐ ☐ ☐
☐ ☐ ☐ ☐ ☐

RATE HOW CLOSELY YOU MET YOUR GOALS TODAY

☐ ☐ ☐ ☐ ☐ ☐ ☐ ☐ ☐ ☐
10% 20% 30% 40% 50% 60% 70% 80% 90% 100%

NOTES:

WEEK 7 FITNESS PLAN

Dates: _____ to _____

	STRENGTH	CARDIO	CLASS / OTHER
MONDAY			
TUESDAY			
WEDNESDAY			
THURSDAY			
FRIDAY			
SATURDAY			
SUNDAY			

WEEK 7 MEAL PLAN

	BREAKFAST	LUNCH	DINNER	SNACKS
MONDAY				
TUESDAY				
WEDNESDAY				
THURSDAY				
FRIDAY				
SATURDAY				
SUNDAY				

DAY 43

Day of the Week | Date: Time:

STRENGTH TRAINING

FOCUS: CHEST ☐ SHOULDERS ☐ BACK ☐ ARMS ☐ LEGS ☐ CORE ☐ NONE ☐   STRETCH/WARM UP: YES ☐ NO ☐

Exercise/Equipment	SET 1		SET 2		SET 3		SET 4	
	REPS	WEIGHT	REPS	WEIGHT	REPS	WEIGHT	REPS	WEIGHT

CARDIO

Exercise / Machine / Class	Duration	Level	Distance	Calories Burned	Heart Rate

OTHER

Exercise / Machine / Class	Duration

NOTES:

NUTRITION

	Food & Beverage	Calories/ Points	Carbs	Fat	Protein	
Breakfast TIME:						
Snack TIME:						
Lunch TIME:						
Snack TIME:						
Dinner TIME:						
Snack TIME:						
Total						

DAILY TARGET TOTALS

Cups of Water ☐☐☐☐☐ ☐☐☐☐☐ ☐☐☐☐☐

Servings of Fruits/ Veggies ☐☐☐☐☐ ☐☐☐☐☐

Hours of Sleep ☐☐☐☐☐ ☐☐☐☐☐

RATE HOW CLOSELY YOU MET YOUR GOALS TODAY

☐ ☐ ☐ ☐ ☐ ☐ ☐ ☐ ☐ ☐
10% 20% 30% 40% 50% 60% 70% 80% 90% 100%

NOTES:

DAY 44

Day of the Week | Date: Time:

STRENGTH TRAINING

FOCUS: CHEST ☐ SHOULDERS ☐ BACK ☐ ARMS ☐ LEGS ☐ CORE ☐ NONE ☐   STRETCH/WARM UP: YES ☐ NO ☐

Exercise/Equipment	SET 1		SET 2		SET 3		SET 4	
	REPS	WEIGHT	REPS	WEIGHT	REPS	WEIGHT	REPS	WEIGHT

CARDIO

Exercise / Machine / Class	Duration	Level	Distance	Calories Burned	Heart Rate

OTHER

Exercise / Machine / Class	Duration

NOTES:

NUTRITION

	Food & Beverage	Calories/ Points	Carbs	Fat	Protein	
Breakfast TIME:						
Snack TIME:						
Lunch TIME:						
Snack TIME:						
Dinner TIME:						
Snack TIME:						
Total						

DAILY TARGET TOTALS

Cups of Water
☐ ☐ ☐ ☐ ☐
☐ ☐ ☐ ☐ ☐
☐ ☐ ☐ ☐ ☐

Servings of Fruits/ Veggies
☐ ☐ ☐ ☐ ☐
☐ ☐ ☐ ☐ ☐

Hours of Sleep
☐ ☐ ☐ ☐ ☐
☐ ☐ ☐ ☐ ☐

RATE HOW CLOSELY YOU MET YOUR GOALS TODAY

☐	☐	☐	☐	☐	☐	☐	☐	☐	☐
10%	20%	30%	40%	50%	60%	70%	80%	90%	100%

NOTES:

_____

_____

_____

DAY 45

Day of the Week | Date: **Time:**

STRENGTH TRAINING

FOCUS: CHEST ☐ SHOULDERS ☐ BACK ☐ ARMS ☐ LEGS ☐ CORE ☐ NONE ☐   STRETCH/WARM UP: YES ☐ NO ☐

Exercise/Equipment	SET 1		SET 2		SET 3		SET 4	
	REPS	WEIGHT	REPS	WEIGHT	REPS	WEIGHT	REPS	WEIGHT

CARDIO

Exercise / Machine / Class	Duration	Level	Distance	Calories Burned	Heart Rate

OTHER

Exercise / Machine / Class	Duration

NOTES:

NUTRITION

	Food & Beverage	Calories/Points	Carbs	Fat	Protein	
Breakfast TIME:						
Snack TIME:						
Lunch TIME:						
Snack TIME:						
Dinner TIME:						
Snack TIME:						
Total						

DAILY TARGET TOTALS

Cups of Water ☐☐☐☐☐ ☐☐☐☐☐ ☐☐☐☐☐

Servings of Fruits/ Veggies ☐☐☐☐☐ ☐☐☐☐☐

Hours of Sleep ☐☐☐☐☐ ☐☐☐☐☐

RATE HOW CLOSELY YOU MET YOUR GOALS TODAY

☐ ☐ ☐ ☐ ☐ ☐ ☐ ☐ ☐ ☐
10% 20% 30% 40% 50% 60% 70% 80% 90% 100%

NOTES:

DAY 46

Day of the Week | Date: Time:

STRENGTH TRAINING

FOCUS: CHEST ☐ SHOULDERS ☐ BACK ☐ ARMS ☐ LEGS ☐ CORE ☐ NONE ☐   STRETCH/WARM UP: YES ☐ NO ☐

Exercise/Equipment	SET 1		SET 2		SET 3		SET 4	
	REPS	WEIGHT	REPS	WEIGHT	REPS	WEIGHT	REPS	WEIGHT

CARDIO

Exercise / Machine / Class	Duration	Level	Distance	Calories Burned	Heart Rate

OTHER

Exercise / Machine / Class	Duration

NOTES:

NUTRITION

	Food & Beverage	Calories/ Points	Carbs	Fat	Protein	
Breakfast TIME:						
Snack TIME:						
Lunch TIME:						
Snack TIME:						
Dinner TIME:						
Snack TIME:						
Total						

DAILY TARGET TOTALS

Cups of Water ☐☐☐☐☐ ☐☐☐☐☐ ☐☐☐☐☐

Servings of Fruits/ Veggies ☐☐☐☐☐ ☐☐☐☐☐

Hours of Sleep ☐☐☐☐☐ ☐☐☐☐☐

RATE HOW CLOSELY YOU MET YOUR GOALS TODAY

☐ ☐ ☐ ☐ ☐ ☐ ☐ ☐ ☐ ☐

10% 20% 30% 40% 50% 60% 70% 80% 90% 100%

NOTES:

_____

_____

_____

_____

DAY 47

Day of the Week | Date: Time:

STRENGTH TRAINING

FOCUS: CHEST ☐ SHOULDERS ☐ BACK ☐ ARMS ☐ LEGS ☐ CORE ☐ NONE ☐   STRETCH/WARM UP: YES ☐ NO ☐

Exercise/Equipment	SET 1		SET 2		SET 3		SET 4	
	REPS	WEIGHT	REPS	WEIGHT	REPS	WEIGHT	REPS	WEIGHT

CARDIO

Exercise / Machine / Class	Duration	Level	Distance	Calories Burned	Heart Rate

OTHER

Exercise / Machine / Class	Duration

NOTES:

NUTRITION

	Food & Beverage	Calories/Points	Carbs	Fat	Protein	
Breakfast TIME:						
Snack TIME:						
Lunch TIME:						
Snack TIME:						
Dinner TIME:						
Snack TIME:						
Total						

DAILY TARGET TOTALS

Cups of Water ☐☐☐☐☐ ☐☐☐☐☐ ☐☐☐☐☐

Servings of Fruits/ Veggies ☐☐☐☐☐ ☐☐☐☐☐

Hours of Sleep ☐☐☐☐☐ ☐☐☐☐☐

RATE HOW CLOSELY YOU MET YOUR GOALS TODAY

☐ ☐ ☐ ☐ ☐ ☐ ☐ ☐ ☐ ☐
10% 20% 30% 40% 50% 60% 70% 80% 90% 100%

NOTES:

DAY 48

Day of the Week | Date: Time:

STRENGTH TRAINING

FOCUS: CHEST ☐ SHOULDERS ☐ BACK ☐ ARMS ☐ LEGS ☐ CORE ☐ NONE ☐   STRETCH/WARM UP: YES ☐ NO ☐

Exercise/Equipment	SET 1		SET 2		SET 3		SET 4	
	REPS	WEIGHT	REPS	WEIGHT	REPS	WEIGHT	REPS	WEIGHT

CARDIO

Exercise / Machine / Class	Duration	Level	Distance	Calories Burned	Heart Rate

OTHER

Exercise / Machine / Class	Duration

NOTES:

	Food & Beverage	Calories/ Points	Carbs	Fat	Protein	
Breakfast TIME:						
Snack TIME:						
Lunch TIME:						
Snack TIME:						
Dinner TIME:						
Snack TIME:						
Total						

DAILY TARGET TOTALS

Cups of Water ☐ ☐ ☐ ☐ ☐ / ☐ ☐ ☐ ☐ ☐ / ☐ ☐ ☐ ☐ ☐

Servings of Fruits/ Veggies ☐ ☐ ☐ ☐ ☐ / ☐ ☐ ☐ ☐ ☐

Hours of Sleep ☐ ☐ ☐ ☐ ☐ / ☐ ☐ ☐ ☐ ☐

RATE HOW CLOSELY YOU MET YOUR GOALS TODAY

☐	☐	☐	☐	☐	☐	☐	☐	☐	☐
10%	20%	30%	40%	50%	60%	70%	80%	90%	100%

NOTES:

DAY 49

Day of the Week | Date: Time:

STRENGTH TRAINING

FOCUS: CHEST ☐ SHOULDERS ☐ BACK ☐ ARMS ☐ LEGS ☐ CORE ☐ NONE ☐   STRETCH/WARM UP: YES ☐ NO ☐

Exercise/Equipment	SET 1		SET 2		SET 3		SET 4	
	REPS	WEIGHT	REPS	WEIGHT	REPS	WEIGHT	REPS	WEIGHT

CARDIO

Exercise / Machine / Class	Duration	Level	Distance	Calories Burned	Heart Rate

OTHER

Exercise / Machine / Class	Duration

NOTES:

NUTRITION

	Food & Beverage	Calories/ Points	Carbs	Fat	Protein	
Breakfast TIME:						
Snack TIME:						
Lunch TIME:						
Snack TIME:						
Dinner TIME:						
Snack TIME:						
Total						

DAILY TARGET TOTALS

Cups of Water ☐☐☐☐☐ ☐☐☐☐☐ ☐☐☐☐☐

Servings of Fruits/ Veggies ☐☐☐☐☐ ☐☐☐☐☐

Hours of Sleep ☐☐☐☐☐ ☐☐☐☐☐

RATE HOW CLOSELY YOU MET YOUR GOALS TODAY

☐	☐	☐	☐	☐	☐	☐	☐	☐	☐
10%	20%	30%	40%	50%	60%	70%	80%	90%	100%

NOTES:

WEEK 8 FITNESS PLAN

Dates: _____ to _____

	STRENGTH	CARDIO	CLASS / OTHER
MONDAY			
TUESDAY			
WEDNESDAY			
THURSDAY			
FRIDAY			
SATURDAY			
SUNDAY			

WEEK 8 MEAL PLAN

	BREAKFAST	LUNCH	DINNER	SNACKS
MONDAY				
TUESDAY				
WEDNESDAY				
THURSDAY				
FRIDAY				
SATURDAY				
SUNDAY				

DAY 50

Day of the Week | Date: Time:

STRENGTH TRAINING

FOCUS: CHEST ☐ SHOULDERS ☐ BACK ☐ ARMS ☐ LEGS ☐ CORE ☐ NONE ☐   STRETCH/WARM UP: YES ☐ NO ☐

Exercise/Equipment	SET 1		SET 2		SET 3		SET 4	
	REPS	WEIGHT	REPS	WEIGHT	REPS	WEIGHT	REPS	WEIGHT

CARDIO

Exercise / Machine / Class	Duration	Level	Distance	Calories Burned	Heart Rate

OTHER

Exercise / Machine / Class	Duration

NOTES:

NUTRITION

	Food & Beverage	Calories/Points	Carbs	Fat	Protein	
Breakfast TIME:						
Snack TIME:						
Lunch TIME:						
Snack TIME:						
Dinner TIME:						
Snack TIME:						
Total						

DAILY TARGET TOTALS

Cups of Water ☐ ☐ ☐ ☐ ☐ ☐ ☐ ☐ ☐ ☐ ☐ ☐ ☐ ☐ ☐

Servings of Fruits/ Veggies ☐ ☐ ☐ ☐ ☐ ☐ ☐ ☐ ☐ ☐

Hours of Sleep ☐ ☐ ☐ ☐ ☐ ☐ ☐ ☐ ☐ ☐

RATE HOW CLOSELY YOU MET YOUR GOALS TODAY

☐	☐	☐	☐	☐	☐	☐	☐	☐	☐
10%	20%	30%	40%	50%	60%	70%	80%	90%	100%

NOTES:

DAY 51

Day of the Week | Date: Time:

STRENGTH TRAINING

FOCUS: CHEST ☐ SHOULDERS ☐ BACK ☐ ARMS ☐ LEGS ☐ CORE ☐ NONE ☐   STRETCH/WARM UP: YES ☐ NO ☐

Exercise/Equipment	SET 1		SET 2		SET 3		SET 4	
	REPS	WEIGHT	REPS	WEIGHT	REPS	WEIGHT	REPS	WEIGHT

CARDIO

Exercise / Machine / Class	Duration	Level	Distance	Calories Burned	Heart Rate

OTHER

Exercise / Machine / Class	Duration

NOTES:

NUTRITION

	Food & Beverage	Calories/ Points	Carbs	Fat	Protein	
Breakfast TIME:						
Snack TIME:						
Lunch TIME:						
Snack TIME:						
Dinner TIME:						
Snack TIME:						
Total						

DAILY TARGET TOTALS

Cups of Water ☐ ☐ ☐ ☐ ☐
☐ ☐ ☐ ☐ ☐
☐ ☐ ☐ ☐ ☐

Servings of Fruits/ Veggies ☐ ☐ ☐ ☐ ☐
☐ ☐ ☐ ☐ ☐

Hours of Sleep ☐ ☐ ☐ ☐ ☐
☐ ☐ ☐ ☐ ☐

RATE HOW CLOSELY YOU MET YOUR GOALS TODAY

☐ ☐ ☐ ☐ ☐ ☐ ☐ ☐ ☐ ☐
10% 20% 30% 40% 50% 60% 70% 80% 90% 100%

NOTES:

DAY 52

Day of the Week | Date: **Time:**

STRENGTH TRAINING

FOCUS: CHEST ☐ SHOULDERS ☐ BACK ☐ ARMS ☐ LEGS ☐ CORE ☐ NONE ☐   STRETCH/WARM UP: YES ☐ NO ☐

Exercise/Equipment	SET 1		SET 2		SET 3		SET 4	
	REPS	WEIGHT	REPS	WEIGHT	REPS	WEIGHT	REPS	WEIGHT

CARDIO

Exercise / Machine / Class	Duration	Level	Distance	Calories Burned	Heart Rate

OTHER

Exercise / Machine / Class	Duration

NOTES:

NUTRITION

	Food & Beverage	Calories/ Points	Carbs	Fat	Protein	
Breakfast TIME:						
Snack TIME:						
Lunch TIME:						
Snack TIME:						
Dinner TIME:						
Snack TIME:						
Total						

DAILY TARGET TOTALS

Cups of Water ☐☐☐☐☐ ☐☐☐☐☐ ☐☐☐☐☐

Servings of Fruits/ Veggies ☐☐☐☐☐ ☐☐☐☐☐

Hours of Sleep ☐☐☐☐☐ ☐☐☐☐☐

RATE HOW CLOSELY YOU MET YOUR GOALS TODAY

☐ ☐ ☐ ☐ ☐ ☐ ☐ ☐ ☐ ☐
10% 20% 30% 40% 50% 60% 70% 80% 90% 100%

NOTES:

DAY 53

Day of the Week | Date: Time:

STRENGTH TRAINING

FOCUS: CHEST ☐ SHOULDERS ☐ BACK ☐ ARMS ☐ LEGS ☐ CORE ☐ NONE ☐   STRETCH/WARM UP: YES ☐ NO ☐

Exercise/Equipment	SET 1		SET 2		SET 3		SET 4	
	REPS	WEIGHT	REPS	WEIGHT	REPS	WEIGHT	REPS	WEIGHT

CARDIO

Exercise / Machine / Class	Duration	Level	Distance	Calories Burned	Heart Rate

OTHER

Exercise / Machine / Class	Duration

NOTES:

	Food & Beverage	Calories/ Points	Carbs	Fat	Protein	
Breakfast TIME:						
Snack TIME:						
Lunch TIME:						
Snack TIME:						
Dinner TIME:						
Snack TIME:						
Total						

DAILY TARGET TOTALS

Cups of Water ☐☐☐☐☐ ☐☐☐☐☐ ☐☐☐☐☐

Servings of Fruits/ Veggies ☐☐☐☐☐ ☐☐☐☐☐

Hours of Sleep ☐☐☐☐☐ ☐☐☐☐☐

RATE HOW CLOSELY YOU MET YOUR GOALS TODAY

☐	☐	☐	☐	☐	☐	☐	☐	☐	☐
10%	20%	30%	40%	50%	60%	70%	80%	90%	100%

NOTES:

_____

_____

_____

DAY 54

Day of the Week | Date: Time:

STRENGTH TRAINING

FOCUS: CHEST ☐ SHOULDERS ☐ BACK ☐ ARMS ☐ LEGS ☐ CORE ☐ NONE ☐   STRETCH/WARM UP: YES ☐ NO ☐

Exercise/Equipment	SET 1		SET 2		SET 3		SET 4	
	REPS	WEIGHT	REPS	WEIGHT	REPS	WEIGHT	REPS	WEIGHT

CARDIO

Exercise / Machine / Class	Duration	Level	Distance	Calories Burned	Heart Rate

OTHER

Exercise / Machine / Class	Duration

NOTES:

NUTRITION

	Food & Beverage	Calories/ Points	Carbs	Fat	Protein	
Breakfast TIME:						
Snack TIME:						
Lunch TIME:						
Snack TIME:						
Dinner TIME:						
Snack TIME:						
Total						

DAILY TARGET TOTALS

Cups of Water ☐ ☐ ☐ ☐ ☐ ☐ ☐ ☐ ☐ ☐ ☐ ☐ ☐ ☐ ☐

Servings of Fruits/ Veggies ☐ ☐ ☐ ☐ ☐ ☐ ☐ ☐ ☐ ☐

Hours of Sleep ☐ ☐ ☐ ☐ ☐ ☐ ☐ ☐ ☐ ☐

RATE HOW CLOSELY YOU MET YOUR GOALS TODAY

☐	☐	☐	☐	☐	☐	☐	☐	☐	☐
10%	20%	30%	40%	50%	60%	70%	80%	90%	100%

NOTES:

_____

_____

_____

DAY 55

Day of the Week | Date: Time:

STRENGTH TRAINING

FOCUS: CHEST ☐ SHOULDERS ☐ BACK ☐ ARMS ☐ LEGS ☐ CORE ☐ NONE ☐   STRETCH/WARM UP: YES ☐ NO ☐

Exercise/Equipment	SET 1		SET 2		SET 3		SET 4	
	REPS	WEIGHT	REPS	WEIGHT	REPS	WEIGHT	REPS	WEIGHT

CARDIO

Exercise / Machine / Class	Duration	Level	Distance	Calories Burned	Heart Rate

OTHER

Exercise / Machine / Class	Duration

NOTES:

NUTRITION

	Food & Beverage	Calories/ Points	Carbs	Fat	Protein	
Breakfast TIME:						
Snack TIME:						
Lunch TIME:						
Snack TIME:						
Dinner TIME:						
Snack TIME:						
Total						

DAILY TARGET TOTALS

Cups of Water ☐ ☐ ☐ ☐ ☐ ☐ ☐ ☐ ☐ ☐ ☐ ☐ ☐ ☐ ☐

Servings of Fruits/ Veggies ☐ ☐ ☐ ☐ ☐ ☐ ☐ ☐ ☐ ☐

Hours of Sleep ☐ ☐ ☐ ☐ ☐ ☐ ☐ ☐ ☐ ☐

RATE HOW CLOSELY YOU MET YOUR GOALS TODAY

☐	☐	☐	☐	☐	☐	☐	☐	☐	☐
10%	20%	30%	40%	50%	60%	70%	80%	90%	100%

NOTES:

DAY 56

Day of the Week | Date: Time:

STRENGTH TRAINING

FOCUS: CHEST ☐ SHOULDERS ☐ BACK ☐ ARMS ☐ LEGS ☐ CORE ☐ NONE ☐   STRETCH/WARM UP: YES ☐ NO ☐

Exercise/Equipment	SET 1		SET 2		SET 3		SET 4	
	REPS	WEIGHT	REPS	WEIGHT	REPS	WEIGHT	REPS	WEIGHT

CARDIO

Exercise / Machine / Class	Duration	Level	Distance	Calories Burned	Heart Rate

OTHER

Exercise / Machine / Class	Duration

NOTES:

NUTRITION

	Food & Beverage	Calories/ Points	Carbs	Fat	Protein	
Breakfast TIME:						
Snack TIME:						
Lunch TIME:						
Snack TIME:						
Dinner TIME:						
Snack TIME:						
Total						

DAILY TARGET TOTALS

Cups of Water ☐☐☐☐☐ ☐☐☐☐☐ ☐☐☐☐☐

Servings of Fruits/ Veggies ☐☐☐☐☐ ☐☐☐☐☐

Hours of Sleep ☐☐☐☐☐ ☐☐☐☐☐

RATE HOW CLOSELY YOU MET YOUR GOALS TODAY

☐	☐	☐	☐	☐	☐	☐	☐	☐	☐
10%	20%	30%	40%	50%	60%	70%	80%	90%	100%

NOTES:

56-DAY CHECK-IN

NOTES

Date:

CURRENT STATS

BODY WEIGHT & MEASUREMENTS

	Current	Goal
Weight		
Body Fat %		
Upper Arms		
Chest		
Waist		
Hips		
Thighs		
Calves		

CARDIO

STRENGTH

ACHIEVING MY GOALS

10%	20%	30%	40%	50%	60%	70%	80%	90%	100%

WEEK 9 FITNESS PLAN

Dates: _____ to _____

	STRENGTH	CARDIO	CLASS / OTHER
MONDAY			
TUESDAY			
WEDNESDAY			
THURSDAY			
FRIDAY			
SATURDAY			
SUNDAY			

WEEK 9 MEAL PLAN

	BREAKFAST	LUNCH	DINNER	SNACKS
MONDAY				
TUESDAY				
WEDNESDAY				
THURSDAY				
FRIDAY				
SATURDAY				
SUNDAY				

DAY 57

Day of the Week | Date: Time:

STRENGTH TRAINING

FOCUS: CHEST ☐ SHOULDERS ☐ BACK ☐ ARMS ☐ LEGS ☐ CORE ☐ NONE ☐   STRETCH/WARM UP: YES ☐ NO ☐

Exercise/Equipment	SET 1		SET 2		SET 3		SET 4	
	REPS	WEIGHT	REPS	WEIGHT	REPS	WEIGHT	REPS	WEIGHT

CARDIO

Exercise / Machine / Class	Duration	Level	Distance	Calories Burned	Heart Rate

OTHER

Exercise / Machine / Class	Duration

NOTES:

NUTRITION

	Food & Beverage	Calories/ Points	Carbs	Fat	Protein	
Breakfast TIME:						
Snack TIME:						
Lunch TIME:						
Snack TIME:						
Dinner TIME:						
Snack TIME:						
Total						

DAILY TARGET TOTALS

Cups of Water ☐ ☐ ☐ ☐ ☐
☐ ☐ ☐ ☐ ☐
☐ ☐ ☐ ☐ ☐

Servings of Fruits/ Veggies ☐ ☐ ☐ ☐ ☐
☐ ☐ ☐ ☐ ☐

Hours of Sleep ☐ ☐ ☐ ☐ ☐
☐ ☐ ☐ ☐ ☐

RATE HOW CLOSELY YOU MET YOUR GOALS TODAY

☐	☐	☐	☐	☐	☐	☐	☐	☐	☐
10%	20%	30%	40%	50%	60%	70%	80%	90%	100%

NOTES:

_____

_____

_____

DAY 58

Day of the Week | Date: _____   Time: _____

STRENGTH TRAINING

FOCUS: CHEST ☐ SHOULDERS ☐ BACK ☐ ARMS ☐ LEGS ☐ CORE ☐ NONE ☐   STRETCH/WARM UP: YES ☐ NO ☐

Exercise/Equipment	SET 1		SET 2		SET 3		SET 4	
	REPS	WEIGHT	REPS	WEIGHT	REPS	WEIGHT	REPS	WEIGHT

CARDIO

Exercise / Machine / Class	Duration	Level	Distance	Calories Burned	Heart Rate

OTHER

Exercise / Machine / Class	Duration

NOTES:

NUTRITION

	Food & Beverage	Calories/ Points	Carbs	Fat	Protein	
Breakfast TIME:						
Snack TIME:						
Lunch TIME:						
Snack TIME:						
Dinner TIME:						
Snack TIME:						
Total						

DAILY TARGET TOTALS

Cups of Water ☐ ☐ ☐ ☐ ☐ ☐ ☐ ☐ ☐ ☐ ☐ ☐ ☐ ☐ ☐

Servings of Fruits/ Veggies ☐ ☐ ☐ ☐ ☐ ☐ ☐ ☐ ☐ ☐

Hours of Sleep ☐ ☐ ☐ ☐ ☐ ☐ ☐ ☐ ☐ ☐

RATE HOW CLOSELY YOU MET YOUR GOALS TODAY

☐ ☐ ☐ ☐ ☐ ☐ ☐ ☐ ☐ ☐
10% 20% 30% 40% 50% 60% 70% 80% 90% 100%

NOTES:

DAY 59

Day of the Week | Date: **Time:**

STRENGTH TRAINING

FOCUS: CHEST ☐ SHOULDERS ☐ BACK ☐ ARMS ☐ LEGS ☐ CORE ☐ NONE ☐   STRETCH/WARM UP: YES ☐ NO ☐

Exercise/Equipment	SET 1		SET 2		SET 3		SET 4	
	REPS	WEIGHT	REPS	WEIGHT	REPS	WEIGHT	REPS	WEIGHT

CARDIO

Exercise / Machine / Class	Duration	Level	Distance	Calories Burned	Heart Rate

OTHER

Exercise / Machine / Class	Duration

NOTES:

NUTRITION

	Food & Beverage	Calories/ Points	Carbs	Fat	Protein	
Breakfast TIME:						
Snack TIME:						
Lunch TIME:						
Snack TIME:						
Dinner TIME:						
Snack TIME:						
Total						

DAILY TARGET TOTALS

Cups of Water ☐☐☐☐☐ ☐☐☐☐☐ ☐☐☐☐☐

Servings of Fruits/ Veggies ☐☐☐☐☐ ☐☐☐☐☐

Hours of Sleep ☐☐☐☐☐ ☐☐☐☐☐

RATE HOW CLOSELY YOU MET YOUR GOALS TODAY

☐ ☐ ☐ ☐ ☐ ☐ ☐ ☐ ☐ ☐
10% 20% 30% 40% 50% 60% 70% 80% 90% 100%

NOTES:

DAY 60

Day of the Week | Date: **Time:**

STRENGTH TRAINING

FOCUS: CHEST ☐ SHOULDERS ☐ BACK ☐ ARMS ☐ LEGS ☐ CORE ☐ NONE ☐   STRETCH/WARM UP: YES ☐ NO ☐

Exercise/Equipment	SET 1		SET 2		SET 3		SET 4	
	REPS	WEIGHT	REPS	WEIGHT	REPS	WEIGHT	REPS	WEIGHT

CARDIO

Exercise / Machine / Class	Duration	Level	Distance	Calories Burned	Heart Rate

OTHER

Exercise / Machine / Class	Duration

NOTES:

NUTRITION

	Food & Beverage	Calories/ Points	Carbs	Fat	Protein	
Breakfast TIME:						
Snack TIME:						
Lunch TIME:						
Snack TIME:						
Dinner TIME:						
Snack TIME:						
Total						

DAILY TARGET TOTALS

Cups of Water	☐ ☐ ☐ ☐ ☐ ☐ ☐ ☐ ☐ ☐ ☐ ☐ ☐ ☐ ☐
Servings of Fruits/ Veggies	☐ ☐ ☐ ☐ ☐ ☐ ☐ ☐ ☐ ☐
Hours of Sleep	☐ ☐ ☐ ☐ ☐ ☐ ☐ ☐ ☐ ☐

RATE HOW CLOSELY YOU MET YOUR GOALS TODAY

☐	☐	☐	☐	☐	☐	☐	☐	☐	☐
10%	20%	30%	40%	50%	60%	70%	80%	90%	100%

NOTES:

DAY 61

Day of the Week | Date: Time:

STRENGTH TRAINING

FOCUS: CHEST ☐ SHOULDERS ☐ BACK ☐ ARMS ☐ LEGS ☐ CORE ☐ NONE ☐   STRETCH/WARM UP: YES ☐ NO ☐

Exercise/Equipment	SET 1		SET 2		SET 3		SET 4	
	REPS	WEIGHT	REPS	WEIGHT	REPS	WEIGHT	REPS	WEIGHT

CARDIO

Exercise / Machine / Class	Duration	Level	Distance	Calories Burned	Heart Rate

OTHER

Exercise / Machine / Class	Duration

NOTES:

NUTRITION

	Food & Beverage	Calories/ Points	Carbs	Fat	Protein	
Breakfast TIME:						
Snack TIME:						
Lunch TIME:						
Snack TIME:						
Dinner TIME:						
Snack TIME:						
Total						

DAILY TARGET TOTALS

Cups of Water	☐ ☐ ☐ ☐ ☐ ☐ ☐ ☐ ☐ ☐ ☐ ☐ ☐ ☐ ☐
Servings of Fruits/ Veggies	☐ ☐ ☐ ☐ ☐ ☐ ☐ ☐ ☐ ☐
Hours of Sleep	☐ ☐ ☐ ☐ ☐ ☐ ☐ ☐ ☐ ☐

RATE HOW CLOSELY YOU MET YOUR GOALS TODAY

☐	☐	☐	☐	☐	☐	☐	☐	☐	☐
10%	20%	30%	40%	50%	60%	70%	80%	90%	100%

NOTES:

DAY 62

Day of the Week | Date: **Time:**

STRENGTH TRAINING

FOCUS: CHEST ☐ SHOULDERS ☐ BACK ☐ ARMS ☐ LEGS ☐ CORE ☐ NONE ☐   STRETCH/WARM UP: YES ☐ NO ☐

Exercise/Equipment	SET 1		SET 2		SET 3		SET 4	
	REPS	WEIGHT	REPS	WEIGHT	REPS	WEIGHT	REPS	WEIGHT

CARDIO

Exercise / Machine / Class	Duration	Level	Distance	Calories Burned	Heart Rate

OTHER

Exercise / Machine / Class	Duration

NOTES:

NUTRITION

	Food & Beverage	Calories/Points	Carbs	Fat	Protein	
Breakfast TIME:						
Snack TIME:						
Lunch TIME:						
Snack TIME:						
Dinner TIME:						
Snack TIME:						
Total						

DAILY TARGET TOTALS

Cups of Water ☐☐☐☐☐ ☐☐☐☐☐ ☐☐☐☐☐

Servings of Fruits/ Veggies ☐☐☐☐☐ ☐☐☐☐☐

Hours of Sleep ☐☐☐☐☐ ☐☐☐☐☐

RATE HOW CLOSELY YOU MET YOUR GOALS TODAY

☐ ☐ ☐ ☐ ☐ ☐ ☐ ☐ ☐ ☐
10% 20% 30% 40% 50% 60% 70% 80% 90% 100%

NOTES:

DAY 63

Day of the Week | Date: Time:

STRENGTH TRAINING

FOCUS: CHEST ☐ SHOULDERS ☐ BACK ☐ ARMS ☐ LEGS ☐ CORE ☐ NONE ☐   STRETCH/WARM UP: YES ☐ NO ☐

Exercise/Equipment	SET 1		SET 2		SET 3		SET 4	
	REPS	WEIGHT	REPS	WEIGHT	REPS	WEIGHT	REPS	WEIGHT

CARDIO

Exercise / Machine / Class	Duration	Level	Distance	Calories Burned	Heart Rate

OTHER

Exercise / Machine / Class	Duration

NOTES:

NUTRITION

	Food & Beverage	Calories/ Points	Carbs	Fat	Protein	
Breakfast TIME:						
Snack TIME:						
Lunch TIME:						
Snack TIME:						
Dinner TIME:						
Snack TIME:						
Total						

DAILY TARGET TOTALS

Cups of Water ☐☐☐☐☐ ☐☐☐☐☐ ☐☐☐☐☐

Servings of Fruits/ Veggies ☐☐☐☐☐ ☐☐☐☐☐

Hours of Sleep ☐☐☐☐☐ ☐☐☐☐☐

RATE HOW CLOSELY YOU MET YOUR GOALS TODAY

☐	☐	☐	☐	☐	☐	☐	☐	☐	☐
10%	20%	30%	40%	50%	60%	70%	80%	90%	100%

NOTES:

WEEK 10 FITNESS PLAN

Dates: _____ to _____

	STRENGTH	CARDIO	CLASS / OTHER
MONDAY			
TUESDAY			
WEDNESDAY			
THURSDAY			
FRIDAY			
SATURDAY			
SUNDAY			

WEEK 10 MEAL PLAN

	BREAKFAST	LUNCH	DINNER	SNACKS
MONDAY				
TUESDAY				
WEDNESDAY				
THURSDAY				
FRIDAY				
SATURDAY				
SUNDAY				

DAY 64

Day of the Week | Date: Time:

STRENGTH TRAINING

FOCUS: CHEST ☐ SHOULDERS ☐ BACK ☐ ARMS ☐ LEGS ☐ CORE ☐ NONE ☐   STRETCH/WARM UP: YES ☐ NO ☐

Exercise/Equipment	SET 1		SET 2		SET 3		SET 4	
	REPS	WEIGHT	REPS	WEIGHT	REPS	WEIGHT	REPS	WEIGHT

CARDIO

Exercise / Machine / Class	Duration	Level	Distance	Calories Burned	Heart Rate

OTHER

Exercise / Machine / Class	Duration

NOTES:

NUTRITION

	Food & Beverage	Calories/Points	Carbs	Fat	Protein	
Breakfast TIME:						
Snack TIME:						
Lunch TIME:						
Snack TIME:						
Dinner TIME:						
Snack TIME:						
Total						

DAILY TARGET TOTALS

Cups of Water ☐☐☐☐☐ ☐☐☐☐☐ ☐☐☐☐☐

Servings of Fruits/ Veggies ☐☐☐☐☐ ☐☐☐☐☐

Hours of Sleep ☐☐☐☐☐ ☐☐☐☐☐

RATE HOW CLOSELY YOU MET YOUR GOALS TODAY

☐ ☐ ☐ ☐ ☐ ☐ ☐ ☐ ☐ ☐
10% 20% 30% 40% 50% 60% 70% 80% 90% 100%

NOTES:

DAY 65

Day of the Week | Date: Time:

STRENGTH TRAINING

FOCUS: CHEST ☐ SHOULDERS ☐ BACK ☐ ARMS ☐ LEGS ☐ CORE ☐ NONE ☐   STRETCH/WARM UP: YES ☐ NO ☐

Exercise/Equipment	SET 1		SET 2		SET 3		SET 4	
	REPS	WEIGHT	REPS	WEIGHT	REPS	WEIGHT	REPS	WEIGHT

CARDIO

Exercise / Machine / Class	Duration	Level	Distance	Calories Burned	Heart Rate

OTHER

Exercise / Machine / Class	Duration

NOTES:

NUTRITION

	Food & Beverage	Calories/ Points	Carbs	Fat	Protein	
Breakfast TIME:						
Snack TIME:						
Lunch TIME:						
Snack TIME:						
Dinner TIME:						
Snack TIME:						
Total						

DAILY TARGET TOTALS

Cups of Water ☐ ☐ ☐ ☐ ☐ ☐ ☐ ☐ ☐ ☐ ☐ ☐ ☐ ☐ ☐

Servings of Fruits/ Veggies ☐ ☐ ☐ ☐ ☐ ☐ ☐ ☐ ☐ ☐

Hours of Sleep ☐ ☐ ☐ ☐ ☐ ☐ ☐ ☐ ☐ ☐

RATE HOW CLOSELY YOU MET YOUR GOALS TODAY

☐ ☐ ☐ ☐ ☐ ☐ ☐ ☐ ☐ ☐
10% 20% 30% 40% 50% 60% 70% 80% 90% 100%

NOTES:

DAY 66

Day of the Week | Date: Time:

STRENGTH TRAINING

FOCUS: CHEST ☐ SHOULDERS ☐ BACK ☐ ARMS ☐ LEGS ☐ CORE ☐ NONE ☐   STRETCH/WARM UP: YES ☐ NO ☐

Exercise/Equipment	SET 1		SET 2		SET 3		SET 4	
	REPS	WEIGHT	REPS	WEIGHT	REPS	WEIGHT	REPS	WEIGHT

CARDIO

Exercise / Machine / Class	Duration	Level	Distance	Calories Burned	Heart Rate

OTHER

Exercise / Machine / Class	Duration

NOTES:

NUTRITION

	Food & Beverage	Calories/ Points	Carbs	Fat	Protein	
Breakfast TIME:						
Snack TIME:						
Lunch TIME:						
Snack TIME:						
Dinner TIME:						
Snack TIME:						
Total						

DAILY TARGET TOTALS

Cups of Water ☐☐☐☐☐ ☐☐☐☐☐ ☐☐☐☐☐

Servings of Fruits/ Veggies ☐☐☐☐☐ ☐☐☐☐☐

Hours of Sleep ☐☐☐☐☐ ☐☐☐☐☐

RATE HOW CLOSELY YOU MET YOUR GOALS TODAY

☐	☐	☐	☐	☐	☐	☐	☐	☐	☐
10%	20%	30%	40%	50%	60%	70%	80%	90%	100%

NOTES:

DAY 67

Day of the Week | Date: Time:

STRENGTH TRAINING

FOCUS: CHEST ☐ SHOULDERS ☐ BACK ☐ ARMS ☐ LEGS ☐ CORE ☐ NONE ☐   STRETCH/WARM UP: YES ☐ NO ☐

Exercise/Equipment	SET 1		SET 2		SET 3		SET 4	
	REPS	WEIGHT	REPS	WEIGHT	REPS	WEIGHT	REPS	WEIGHT

CARDIO

Exercise / Machine / Class	Duration	Level	Distance	Calories Burned	Heart Rate

OTHER

Exercise / Machine / Class	Duration

NOTES:

NUTRITION

	Food & Beverage	Calories/Points	Carbs	Fat	Protein	
Breakfast TIME:						
Snack TIME:						
Lunch TIME:						
Snack TIME:						
Dinner TIME:						
Snack TIME:						
Total						

DAILY TARGET TOTALS

Cups of Water	☐ ☐ ☐ ☐ ☐ ☐ ☐ ☐ ☐ ☐ ☐ ☐ ☐ ☐ ☐
Servings of Fruits/ Veggies	☐ ☐ ☐ ☐ ☐ ☐ ☐ ☐ ☐ ☐
Hours of Sleep	☐ ☐ ☐ ☐ ☐ ☐ ☐ ☐ ☐ ☐

RATE HOW CLOSELY YOU MET YOUR GOALS TODAY

☐	☐	☐	☐	☐	☐	☐	☐	☐	☐
10%	20%	30%	40%	50%	60%	70%	80%	90%	100%

NOTES:

DAY 68

Day of the Week | Date: Time:

STRENGTH TRAINING

FOCUS: CHEST ☐ SHOULDERS ☐ BACK ☐ ARMS ☐ LEGS ☐ CORE ☐ NONE ☐   STRETCH/WARM UP: YES ☐ NO ☐

Exercise/Equipment	SET 1		SET 2		SET 3		SET 4	
	REPS	WEIGHT	REPS	WEIGHT	REPS	WEIGHT	REPS	WEIGHT

CARDIO

Exercise / Machine / Class	Duration	Level	Distance	Calories Burned	Heart Rate

OTHER

Exercise / Machine / Class	Duration

NOTES:

NUTRITION

	Food & Beverage	Calories/ Points	Carbs	Fat	Protein	
Breakfast TIME:						
Snack TIME:						
Lunch TIME:						
Snack TIME:						
Dinner TIME:						
Snack TIME:						
Total						

DAILY TARGET TOTALS

Cups of Water ☐☐☐☐☐ ☐☐☐☐☐ ☐☐☐☐☐

Servings of Fruits/ Veggies ☐☐☐☐☐ ☐☐☐☐☐

Hours of Sleep ☐☐☐☐☐ ☐☐☐☐☐

RATE HOW CLOSELY YOU MET YOUR GOALS TODAY

☐ ☐ ☐ ☐ ☐ ☐ ☐ ☐ ☐ ☐
10% 20% 30% 40% 50% 60% 70% 80% 90% 100%

NOTES:

DAY 69

Day of the Week | Date: Time:

STRENGTH TRAINING

FOCUS: CHEST ☐ SHOULDERS ☐ BACK ☐ ARMS ☐ LEGS ☐ CORE ☐ NONE ☐   STRETCH/WARM UP: YES ☐ NO ☐

Exercise/Equipment	SET 1		SET 2		SET 3		SET 4	
	REPS	WEIGHT	REPS	WEIGHT	REPS	WEIGHT	REPS	WEIGHT

CARDIO

Exercise / Machine / Class	Duration	Level	Distance	Calories Burned	Heart Rate

OTHER

Exercise / Machine / Class	Duration

NOTES:

NUTRITION

	Food & Beverage	Calories/ Points	Carbs	Fat	Protein	
Breakfast TIME:						
Snack TIME:						
Lunch TIME:						
Snack TIME:						
Dinner TIME:						
Snack TIME:						
Total						

DAILY TARGET TOTALS

Cups of Water ☐☐☐☐☐ ☐☐☐☐☐ ☐☐☐☐☐

Servings of Fruits/ Veggies ☐☐☐☐☐ ☐☐☐☐☐

Hours of Sleep ☐☐☐☐☐ ☐☐☐☐☐

RATE HOW CLOSELY YOU MET YOUR GOALS TODAY

☐ ☐ ☐ ☐ ☐ ☐ ☐ ☐ ☐ ☐
10% 20% 30% 40% 50% 60% 70% 80% 90% 100%

NOTES:

DAY 70

Day of the Week | Date: Time:

STRENGTH TRAINING

FOCUS: CHEST ☐ SHOULDERS ☐ BACK ☐ ARMS ☐ LEGS ☐ CORE ☐ NONE ☐   STRETCH/WARM UP: YES ☐ NO ☐

Exercise/Equipment	SET 1		SET 2		SET 3		SET 4	
	REPS	WEIGHT	REPS	WEIGHT	REPS	WEIGHT	REPS	WEIGHT

CARDIO

Exercise / Machine / Class	Duration	Level	Distance	Calories Burned	Heart Rate

OTHER

Exercise / Machine / Class	Duration

NOTES:

NUTRITION

	Food & Beverage	Calories/ Points	Carbs	Fat	Protein	
Breakfast TIME:						
Snack TIME:						
Lunch TIME:						
Snack TIME:						
Dinner TIME:						
Snack TIME:						
Total						

DAILY TARGET TOTALS

Cups of Water ☐☐☐☐☐ ☐☐☐☐☐ ☐☐☐☐☐

Servings of Fruits/ Veggies ☐☐☐☐☐ ☐☐☐☐☐

Hours of Sleep ☐☐☐☐☐ ☐☐☐☐☐

RATE HOW CLOSELY YOU MET YOUR GOALS TODAY

☐	☐	☐	☐	☐	☐	☐	☐	☐	☐
10%	20%	30%	40%	50%	60%	70%	80%	90%	100%

NOTES:

_____

_____

_____

_____

WEEK 11 FITNESS PLAN

Dates: _____ to _____

	STRENGTH	CARDIO	CLASS / OTHER
MONDAY			
TUESDAY			
WEDNESDAY			
THURSDAY			
FRIDAY			
SATURDAY			
SUNDAY			

WEEK 11 MEAL PLAN

	BREAKFAST	LUNCH	DINNER	SNACKS
MONDAY				
TUESDAY				
WEDNESDAY				
THURSDAY				
FRIDAY				
SATURDAY				
SUNDAY				

DAY 71

Day of the Week | Date: Time:

STRENGTH TRAINING

FOCUS: CHEST ☐ SHOULDERS ☐ BACK ☐ ARMS ☐ LEGS ☐ CORE ☐ NONE ☐   STRETCH/WARM UP: YES ☐ NO ☐

Exercise/Equipment	SET 1		SET 2		SET 3		SET 4	
	REPS	WEIGHT	REPS	WEIGHT	REPS	WEIGHT	REPS	WEIGHT

CARDIO

Exercise / Machine / Class	Duration	Level	Distance	Calories Burned	Heart Rate

OTHER

Exercise / Machine / Class	Duration

NOTES:

NUTRITION

	Food & Beverage	Calories/Points	Carbs	Fat	Protein	
Breakfast TIME:						
Snack TIME:						
Lunch TIME:						
Snack TIME:						
Dinner TIME:						
Snack TIME:						
Total						

DAILY TARGET TOTALS

Cups of Water ☐☐☐☐☐ ☐☐☐☐☐ ☐☐☐☐☐

Servings of Fruits/ Veggies ☐☐☐☐☐ ☐☐☐☐☐

Hours of Sleep ☐☐☐☐☐ ☐☐☐☐☐

RATE HOW CLOSELY YOU MET YOUR GOALS TODAY

☐	☐	☐	☐	☐	☐	☐	☐	☐	☐
10%	20%	30%	40%	50%	60%	70%	80%	90%	100%

NOTES:

DAY 72

Day of the Week | Date: Time:

STRENGTH TRAINING

FOCUS: CHEST ☐ SHOULDERS ☐ BACK ☐ ARMS ☐ LEGS ☐ CORE ☐ NONE ☐   STRETCH/WARM UP: YES ☐ NO ☐

Exercise/Equipment	SET 1		SET 2		SET 3		SET 4	
	REPS	WEIGHT	REPS	WEIGHT	REPS	WEIGHT	REPS	WEIGHT

CARDIO

Exercise / Machine / Class	Duration	Level	Distance	Calories Burned	Heart Rate

OTHER

Exercise / Machine / Class	Duration

NOTES:

NUTRITION

	Food & Beverage	Calories/ Points	Carbs	Fat	Protein	
Breakfast TIME:						
Snack TIME:						
Lunch TIME:						
Snack TIME:						
Dinner TIME:						
Snack TIME:						
Total						

DAILY TARGET TOTALS

Cups of Water ☐ ☐ ☐ ☐ ☐ ☐ ☐ ☐ ☐ ☐ ☐ ☐ ☐ ☐ ☐

Servings of Fruits/ Veggies ☐ ☐ ☐ ☐ ☐ ☐ ☐ ☐ ☐ ☐

Hours of Sleep ☐ ☐ ☐ ☐ ☐ ☐ ☐ ☐ ☐ ☐

RATE HOW CLOSELY YOU MET YOUR GOALS TODAY

☐ ☐ ☐ ☐ ☐ ☐ ☐ ☐ ☐ ☐
10% 20% 30% 40% 50% 60% 70% 80% 90% 100%

NOTES:

DAY 73

Day of the Week | Date: Time:

STRENGTH TRAINING

FOCUS: CHEST ☐ SHOULDERS ☐ BACK ☐ ARMS ☐ LEGS ☐ CORE ☐ NONE ☐   STRETCH/WARM UP: YES ☐ NO ☐

Exercise/Equipment	SET 1		SET 2		SET 3		SET 4	
	REPS	WEIGHT	REPS	WEIGHT	REPS	WEIGHT	REPS	WEIGHT

CARDIO

Exercise / Machine / Class	Duration	Level	Distance	Calories Burned	Heart Rate

OTHER

Exercise / Machine / Class	Duration

NOTES:

NUTRITION

	Food & Beverage	Calories/ Points	Carbs	Fat	Protein	
Breakfast TIME:						
Snack TIME:						
Lunch TIME:						
Snack TIME:						
Dinner TIME:						
Snack TIME:						
Total						

DAILY TARGET TOTALS

Cups of Water ☐☐☐☐☐ ☐☐☐☐☐ ☐☐☐☐☐

Servings of Fruits/ Veggies ☐☐☐☐☐ ☐☐☐☐☐

Hours of Sleep ☐☐☐☐☐ ☐☐☐☐☐

RATE HOW CLOSELY YOU MET YOUR GOALS TODAY

☐ ☐ ☐ ☐ ☐ ☐ ☐ ☐ ☐ ☐
10% 20% 30% 40% 50% 60% 70% 80% 90% 100%

NOTES:

DAY 74

Day of the Week | Date: Time:

STRENGTH TRAINING

FOCUS: CHEST ☐ SHOULDERS ☐ BACK ☐ ARMS ☐ LEGS ☐ CORE ☐ NONE ☐   STRETCH/WARM UP: YES ☐ NO ☐

Exercise/Equipment	SET 1		SET 2		SET 3		SET 4	
	REPS	WEIGHT	REPS	WEIGHT	REPS	WEIGHT	REPS	WEIGHT

CARDIO

Exercise / Machine / Class	Duration	Level	Distance	Calories Burned	Heart Rate

OTHER

Exercise / Machine / Class	Duration

NOTES:

NUTRITION

	Food & Beverage	Calories/ Points	Carbs	Fat	Protein	
Breakfast TIME:						
Snack TIME:						
Lunch TIME:						
Snack TIME:						
Dinner TIME:						
Snack TIME:						
Total						

DAILY TARGET TOTALS

Cups of Water ☐☐☐☐☐ ☐☐☐☐☐ ☐☐☐☐☐

Servings of Fruits/ Veggies ☐☐☐☐☐ ☐☐☐☐☐

Hours of Sleep ☐☐☐☐☐ ☐☐☐☐☐

RATE HOW CLOSELY YOU MET YOUR GOALS TODAY

☐ ☐ ☐ ☐ ☐ ☐ ☐ ☐ ☐ ☐
10% 20% 30% 40% 50% 60% 70% 80% 90% 100%

NOTES:

DAY 75

Day of the Week | Date: Time:

STRENGTH TRAINING

FOCUS: CHEST ☐ SHOULDERS ☐ BACK ☐ ARMS ☐ LEGS ☐ CORE ☐ NONE ☐   STRETCH/WARM UP: YES ☐ NO ☐

Exercise/Equipment	SET 1		SET 2		SET 3		SET 4	
	REPS	WEIGHT	REPS	WEIGHT	REPS	WEIGHT	REPS	WEIGHT

CARDIO

Exercise / Machine / Class	Duration	Level	Distance	Calories Burned	Heart Rate

OTHER

Exercise / Machine / Class	Duration

NOTES:

NUTRITION

	Food & Beverage	Calories/ Points	Carbs	Fat	Protein	
Breakfast TIME:						
Snack TIME:						
Lunch TIME:						
Snack TIME:						
Dinner TIME:						
Snack TIME:						
Total						

DAILY TARGET TOTALS

Cups of Water
☐ ☐ ☐ ☐ ☐
☐ ☐ ☐ ☐ ☐
☐ ☐ ☐ ☐ ☐

Servings of Fruits/ Veggies
☐ ☐ ☐ ☐ ☐
☐ ☐ ☐ ☐ ☐

Hours of Sleep
☐ ☐ ☐ ☐ ☐
☐ ☐ ☐ ☐ ☐

RATE HOW CLOSELY YOU MET YOUR GOALS TODAY

☐ ☐ ☐ ☐ ☐ ☐ ☐ ☐ ☐ ☐
10% 20% 30% 40% 50% 60% 70% 80% 90% 100%

NOTES:

DAY 76

Day of the Week | Date: Time:

STRENGTH TRAINING

FOCUS: CHEST ☐ SHOULDERS ☐ BACK ☐ ARMS ☐ LEGS ☐ CORE ☐ NONE ☐   STRETCH/WARM UP: YES ☐ NO ☐

Exercise/Equipment	SET 1		SET 2		SET 3		SET 4	
	REPS	WEIGHT	REPS	WEIGHT	REPS	WEIGHT	REPS	WEIGHT

CARDIO

Exercise / Machine / Class	Duration	Level	Distance	Calories Burned	Heart Rate

OTHER

Exercise / Machine / Class	Duration

NOTES:

	Food & Beverage	Calories/ Points	Carbs	Fat	Protein	
Breakfast TIME:						
Snack TIME:						
Lunch TIME:						
Snack TIME:						
Dinner TIME:						
Snack TIME:						
Total						

DAILY TARGET TOTALS

Cups of Water ☐☐☐☐☐ ☐☐☐☐☐ ☐☐☐☐☐

Servings of Fruits/ Veggies ☐☐☐☐☐ ☐☐☐☐☐

Hours of Sleep ☐☐☐☐☐ ☐☐☐☐☐

RATE HOW CLOSELY YOU MET YOUR GOALS TODAY

☐ ☐ ☐ ☐ ☐ ☐ ☐ ☐ ☐ ☐
10% 20% 30% 40% 50% 60% 70% 80% 90% 100%

NOTES:

DAY 77

Day of the Week | Date: Time:

STRENGTH TRAINING

FOCUS: CHEST ☐ SHOULDERS ☐ BACK ☐ ARMS ☐ LEGS ☐ CORE ☐ NONE ☐   STRETCH/WARM UP: YES ☐ NO ☐

Exercise/Equipment	SET 1		SET 2		SET 3		SET 4	
	REPS	WEIGHT	REPS	WEIGHT	REPS	WEIGHT	REPS	WEIGHT

CARDIO

Exercise / Machine / Class	Duration	Level	Distance	Calories Burned	Heart Rate

OTHER

Exercise / Machine / Class	Duration

NOTES:

	Food & Beverage	Calories/Points	Carbs	Fat	Protein	
Breakfast TIME:						
Snack TIME:						
Lunch TIME:						
Snack TIME:						
Dinner TIME:						
Snack TIME:						
Total						

DAILY TARGET TOTALS

Cups of Water ☐☐☐☐☐ ☐☐☐☐☐ ☐☐☐☐☐

Servings of Fruits/ Veggies ☐☐☐☐☐ ☐☐☐☐☐

Hours of Sleep ☐☐☐☐☐ ☐☐☐☐☐

RATE HOW CLOSELY YOU MET YOUR GOALS TODAY

☐	☐	☐	☐	☐	☐	☐	☐	☐	☐
10%	20%	30%	40%	50%	60%	70%	80%	90%	100%

NOTES:

WEEK 12 FITNESS PLAN

Dates: _____ to _____

	STRENGTH	CARDIO	CLASS / OTHER
MONDAY			
TUESDAY			
WEDNESDAY			
THURSDAY			
FRIDAY			
SATURDAY			
SUNDAY			

WEEK 12 MEAL PLAN

	BREAKFAST	LUNCH	DINNER	SNACKS
MONDAY				
TUESDAY				
WEDNESDAY				
THURSDAY				
FRIDAY				
SATURDAY				
SUNDAY				

DAY 78

Day of the Week | Date: Time:

STRENGTH TRAINING

FOCUS: CHEST ☐ SHOULDERS ☐ BACK ☐ ARMS ☐ LEGS ☐ CORE ☐ NONE ☐   STRETCH/WARM UP: YES ☐ NO ☐

Exercise/Equipment	SET 1		SET 2		SET 3		SET 4	
	REPS	WEIGHT	REPS	WEIGHT	REPS	WEIGHT	REPS	WEIGHT

CARDIO

Exercise / Machine / Class	Duration	Level	Distance	Calories Burned	Heart Rate

OTHER

Exercise / Machine / Class	Duration

NOTES:

NUTRITION

	Food & Beverage	Calories/ Points	Carbs	Fat	Protein	
Breakfast TIME:						
Snack TIME:						
Lunch TIME:						
Snack TIME:						
Dinner TIME:						
Snack TIME:						
Total						

DAILY TARGET TOTALS

Cups of Water ☐ ☐ ☐ ☐ ☐ ☐ ☐ ☐ ☐ ☐ ☐ ☐ ☐ ☐ ☐

Servings of Fruits/ Veggies ☐ ☐ ☐ ☐ ☐ ☐ ☐ ☐ ☐ ☐

Hours of Sleep ☐ ☐ ☐ ☐ ☐ ☐ ☐ ☐ ☐ ☐

RATE HOW CLOSELY YOU MET YOUR GOALS TODAY

☐ ☐ ☐ ☐ ☐ ☐ ☐ ☐ ☐ ☐
10% 20% 30% 40% 50% 60% 70% 80% 90% 100%

NOTES:

DAY 79

Day of the Week | Date: Time:

STRENGTH TRAINING

FOCUS: CHEST ☐ SHOULDERS ☐ BACK ☐ ARMS ☐ LEGS ☐ CORE ☐ NONE ☐   STRETCH/WARM UP: YES ☐ NO ☐

Exercise/Equipment	SET 1		SET 2		SET 3		SET 4	
	REPS	WEIGHT	REPS	WEIGHT	REPS	WEIGHT	REPS	WEIGHT

CARDIO

Exercise / Machine / Class	Duration	Level	Distance	Calories Burned	Heart Rate

OTHER

Exercise / Machine / Class	Duration

NOTES:

NUTRITION

	Food & Beverage	Calories/ Points	Carbs	Fat	Protein	
Breakfast TIME:						
Snack TIME:						
Lunch TIME:						
Snack TIME:						
Dinner TIME:						
Snack TIME:						
Total						

DAILY TARGET TOTALS

Cups of Water ☐☐☐☐☐ ☐☐☐☐☐ ☐☐☐☐☐

Servings of Fruits/ Veggies ☐☐☐☐☐ ☐☐☐☐☐

Hours of Sleep ☐☐☐☐☐ ☐☐☐☐☐

RATE HOW CLOSELY YOU MET YOUR GOALS TODAY

☐ ☐ ☐ ☐ ☐ ☐ ☐ ☐ ☐ ☐
10% 20% 30% 40% 50% 60% 70% 80% 90% 100%

NOTES:

DAY 80

Day of the Week | Date: Time:

STRENGTH TRAINING

FOCUS: CHEST ☐ SHOULDERS ☐ BACK ☐ ARMS ☐ LEGS ☐ CORE ☐ NONE ☐   STRETCH/WARM UP: YES ☐ NO ☐

Exercise/Equipment	SET 1		SET 2		SET 3		SET 4	
	REPS	WEIGHT	REPS	WEIGHT	REPS	WEIGHT	REPS	WEIGHT

CARDIO

Exercise / Machine / Class	Duration	Level	Distance	Calories Burned	Heart Rate

OTHER

Exercise / Machine / Class	Duration

NOTES:

NUTRITION

	Food & Beverage	Calories/ Points	Carbs	Fat	Protein	
Breakfast TIME:						
Snack TIME:						
Lunch TIME:						
Snack TIME:						
Dinner TIME:						
Snack TIME:						
Total						

DAILY TARGET TOTALS

Cups of Water ☐ ☐ ☐ ☐ ☐ ☐ ☐ ☐ ☐ ☐ ☐ ☐ ☐ ☐ ☐

Servings of Fruits/ Veggies ☐ ☐ ☐ ☐ ☐ ☐ ☐ ☐ ☐ ☐

Hours of Sleep ☐ ☐ ☐ ☐ ☐ ☐ ☐ ☐ ☐ ☐

RATE HOW CLOSELY YOU MET YOUR GOALS TODAY

☐	☐	☐	☐	☐	☐	☐	☐	☐	☐
10%	20%	30%	40%	50%	60%	70%	80%	90%	100%

NOTES:

_____

_____

_____

DAY 81

Day of the Week | Date: Time:

STRENGTH TRAINING

FOCUS: CHEST ☐ SHOULDERS ☐ BACK ☐ ARMS ☐ LEGS ☐ CORE ☐ NONE ☐   STRETCH/WARM UP: YES ☐ NO ☐

Exercise/Equipment	SET 1		SET 2		SET 3		SET 4	
	REPS	WEIGHT	REPS	WEIGHT	REPS	WEIGHT	REPS	WEIGHT

CARDIO

Exercise / Machine / Class	Duration	Level	Distance	Calories Burned	Heart Rate

OTHER

Exercise / Machine / Class	Duration

NOTES:

NUTRITION

	Food & Beverage	Calories/ Points	Carbs	Fat	Protein	
Breakfast TIME:						
Snack TIME:						
Lunch TIME:						
Snack TIME:						
Dinner TIME:						
Snack TIME:						
Total						

DAILY TARGET TOTALS

Cups of Water ☐ ☐ ☐ ☐ ☐ ☐ ☐ ☐ ☐ ☐ ☐ ☐ ☐ ☐ ☐

Servings of Fruits/ Veggies ☐ ☐ ☐ ☐ ☐ ☐ ☐ ☐ ☐ ☐

Hours of Sleep ☐ ☐ ☐ ☐ ☐ ☐ ☐ ☐ ☐ ☐

RATE HOW CLOSELY YOU MET YOUR GOALS TODAY

☐ ☐ ☐ ☐ ☐ ☐ ☐ ☐ ☐ ☐
10% 20% 30% 40% 50% 60% 70% 80% 90% 100%

NOTES:

DAY 82

Day of the Week | Date: Time:

STRENGTH TRAINING

FOCUS: CHEST ☐ SHOULDERS ☐ BACK ☐ ARMS ☐ LEGS ☐ CORE ☐ NONE ☐   STRETCH/WARM UP: YES ☐ NO ☐

Exercise/Equipment	SET 1		SET 2		SET 3		SET 4	
	REPS	WEIGHT	REPS	WEIGHT	REPS	WEIGHT	REPS	WEIGHT

CARDIO

Exercise / Machine / Class	Duration	Level	Distance	Calories Burned	Heart Rate

OTHER

Exercise / Machine / Class	Duration

NOTES:

NUTRITION

	Food & Beverage	Calories/ Points	Carbs	Fat	Protein	
Breakfast TIME:						
Snack TIME:						
Lunch TIME:						
Snack TIME:						
Dinner TIME:						
Snack TIME:						
Total						

DAILY TARGET TOTALS

Cups of Water ☐ ☐ ☐ ☐ ☐ ☐ ☐ ☐ ☐ ☐ ☐ ☐ ☐ ☐ ☐

Servings of Fruits/ Veggies ☐ ☐ ☐ ☐ ☐ ☐ ☐ ☐ ☐ ☐

Hours of Sleep ☐ ☐ ☐ ☐ ☐ ☐ ☐ ☐ ☐ ☐

RATE HOW CLOSELY YOU MET YOUR GOALS TODAY

☐	☐	☐	☐	☐	☐	☐	☐	☐	☐
10%	20%	30%	40%	50%	60%	70%	80%	90%	100%

NOTES:

_____

_____

_____

DAY 83

Day of the Week | Date: Time:

STRENGTH TRAINING

FOCUS: CHEST ☐ SHOULDERS ☐ BACK ☐ ARMS ☐ LEGS ☐ CORE ☐ NONE ☐   STRETCH/WARM UP: YES ☐ NO ☐

Exercise/Equipment	SET 1		SET 2		SET 3		SET 4	
	REPS	WEIGHT	REPS	WEIGHT	REPS	WEIGHT	REPS	WEIGHT

CARDIO

Exercise / Machine / Class	Duration	Level	Distance	Calories Burned	Heart Rate

OTHER

Exercise / Machine / Class	Duration

NOTES:

NUTRITION

	Food & Beverage	Calories/ Points	Carbs	Fat	Protein	
Breakfast TIME:						
Snack TIME:						
Lunch TIME:						
Snack TIME:						
Dinner TIME:						
Snack TIME:						
Total						

DAILY TARGET TOTALS

Cups of Water ☐☐☐☐☐ ☐☐☐☐☐ ☐☐☐☐☐

Servings of Fruits/ Veggies ☐☐☐☐☐ ☐☐☐☐☐

Hours of Sleep ☐☐☐☐☐ ☐☐☐☐☐

RATE HOW CLOSELY YOU MET YOUR GOALS TODAY

☐ ☐ ☐ ☐ ☐ ☐ ☐ ☐ ☐ ☐
10% 20% 30% 40% 50% 60% 70% 80% 90% 100%

NOTES:

DAY 84

Day of the Week | Date: Time:

STRENGTH TRAINING

FOCUS: CHEST ☐ SHOULDERS ☐ BACK ☐ ARMS ☐ LEGS ☐ CORE ☐ NONE ☐   STRETCH/WARM UP: YES ☐ NO ☐

Exercise/Equipment	SET 1		SET 2		SET 3		SET 4	
	REPS	WEIGHT	REPS	WEIGHT	REPS	WEIGHT	REPS	WEIGHT

CARDIO

Exercise / Machine / Class	Duration	Level	Distance	Calories Burned	Heart Rate

OTHER

Exercise / Machine / Class	Duration

NOTES:

NUTRITION

	Food & Beverage	Calories/ Points	Carbs	Fat	Protein	
Breakfast TIME:						
Snack TIME:						
Lunch TIME:						
Snack TIME:						
Dinner TIME:						
Snack TIME:						
Total						

DAILY TARGET TOTALS

Cups of Water ☐ ☐ ☐ ☐ ☐ ☐ ☐ ☐ ☐ ☐ ☐ ☐ ☐ ☐ ☐

Servings of Fruits/ Veggies ☐ ☐ ☐ ☐ ☐ ☐ ☐ ☐ ☐ ☐

Hours of Sleep ☐ ☐ ☐ ☐ ☐ ☐ ☐ ☐ ☐ ☐

RATE HOW CLOSELY YOU MET YOUR GOALS TODAY

☐	☐	☐	☐	☐	☐	☐	☐	☐	☐
10%	20%	30%	40%	50%	60%	70%	80%	90%	100%

NOTES:

FINAL CHECK-IN

NOTES

Date: